Journey's End

GCSE Student Guide

Methuen Drama publications for GCSE students

Available and forthcoming

GCSE Student Editions

Willy Russell's *Blood Brothers*
Simon Stephens's *The Curious Incident of the Dog in the Night-Time*
Charlotte Keatley's *My Mother Said I Never Should*
Shelagh Delaney's *A Taste of Honey*

GCSE Student Guides

Willy Russell's *Blood Brothers* by Ros Merkin
Simon Stephens's *The Curious Incident of the Dog in the Night-Time* by Jacqueline Bolton
Dennis Kelly's *DNA* by Maggie Inchley
Alan Bennett's *The History Boys* by Steve Nicholson
J. B. Priestley's *An Inspector Calls* by Philip Roberts
R. C. Sherriff's *Journey's End* by Andrew Maunder
Charlotte Keatley's *My Mother Said I Never Should* by Sophie Bush
Shelagh Delaney's *A Taste of Honey* by Kate Whittaker

Journey's End GCSE Student Guide

ANDREW MAUNDER

Series Editor: Jenny Stevens

Bloomsbury Methuen Drama
An imprint of Bloomsbury Publishing Plc

B L O O M S B U R Y
LONDON · OXFORD · NEW YORK · NEW DELHI · SYDNEY

Bloomsbury Methuen Drama

An imprint of Bloomsbury Publishing Plc

Imprint previously known as Methuen Drama

50 Bedford Square
London
WC1B 3DP
UK

1385 Broadway
New York
NY 10018
USA

www.bloomsbury.com

BLOOMSBURY, METHUEN DRAMA and the Diana logo are trademarks of Bloomsbury Publishing Plc

British Library Cataloguing-in-Publication Data
A catalogue record for this book is available from the British Library.

ISBN:	PB:	978-1-4742-3228-9
	ePDF:	978-1-4742-3229-6
	epub:	978-1-4742-3230-2

Library of Congress Cataloging-in-Publication Data
A catalog record for this book is available from the Library of Congress.

Series: GSCE Student Guides

Typeset by RefineCatch Limited, Bungay, Suffolk
Printed and bound in Great Britain

CONTENTS

CHAPTER ONE

The Play

Introduction

Journey's End is a three-act play by R[obert] C[edric] Sherriff (1896–1975). It has an all-male cast. Its events take place in an officers' dugout attached to the British trenches at St Quentin in Picardy, in northern France, in the days preceding the German army's offensive of March 1918 in the last year of the First World War (1914–1918). Since its first staging in 1928, *Journey's End* has become part of the *canon* of First World War literature and is regularly performed.[1] Claims for the play's importance have appeared in a multitude of settings and it is read, taught and performed throughout the world, and its presence felt in many different locations.

Why is *Journey's End* an important play? Answers to this question fluctuate wildly. There is *Journey's End*, the anti-war play which has shown each new generation the sacrifices made in, and damage wrought by, the First World War. It is this *Journey's End*, for example, which in the midst of the First World War Centenary beginning in 2014, prompts pleas for its relevance at time of 'increasing awareness of the damage to young people who fight for their country, and survive' (*Oxford*

---

[1] A 'canon' of literary texts is comprised of texts widely agreed by critics and educational authorities to be important.

Times, 25 September 2014). There is another *Journey's End* – the snobbish, reactionary play focused on public-school educated young men and which articulates numerous anxieties – fears of women, of the working-classes, of homosexuality disguised as male-bonding. Then there is the play which deals very movingly in universal, timeless issues, fundamental human emotions – love, selflessness, friendship, self-sacrifice, bravery. Whatever one's take on it, what is certainly true is that these different views of *Journey's End* set the terms for a critical debate that is still being played out and is certainly set to continue – and in which you, as a critic, are being invited to participate in this guide.

Reading a play

You will know that reading a play is not the same as reading a novel. In a useful book, *Studying Plays* (1998), Simon Shepherd and Mick Wallis make the point that a printed version of a play is always 'a strange – incomplete – object'. They go on: 'The business of reading a play is rather unsatisfactory because we continually have the sense that what we are looking at is only words on a page, and that those words have yet to come alive in the mouths of real human beings standing on a stage' (1–2). This argument is as true for *Journey's End* as much as for any play. When picking up our printed copy we need to use our imagination, we have to *visualize*. In particular, we need to pay attention to the following.

Stage directions (the words in *italics* indicating movement and physical response). Stage directions are important for giving information to the actor (and director) about when and how characters move. They can also suggest emotion and mood (anger, unhappiness, joy, hate, etc.). They can indicate power relations between characters. Do characters stand up or sit down in each other's presence? Do they bow or salute each other? Stage directions can also indicate vital aspects of characters' feelings towards each other. One way of acknowledging them is to have one person reading the stage directions when your group reads the play aloud. You should also think about how you – if asked to direct the play – would want actors to interpret particular gestures and lines.

Setting (where the events takes place). It is evident that R.C. Sherriff was also very interested in the 'look' of the play, not least how the environment, 'a squalid cavern in the ground' as he put it, impacts on the behaviour of his characters (*No Leading Lady*, 47). The choice of a dugout as the play's setting was significant in another way. A dugout, Sherriff explained was 'the perfect natural setting' for a play. He continued:

> It [the dugout that he remembered from serving in the army] was usually one of a chain of dugouts linked together by short tunnels, each with its own way up to the trench by a steep flight of steps. The tunnel to one side would lead to the dugout where some of the officers slept, the opposite one to ... the place where the cook-batman prepared the meals. This made it easy to move the characters in and out as needed. An officer would go up the steps to take his turn of duty in the trenches: the one he relieved would come in for a meal, and then go off stage to the adjoining dugout for some sleep when he was no longer required. With a little simple planning you could bring the characters together and disperse them easily (35–6).

Dialogue (the words spoken by the characters). Dialogue has several functions. It helps the audience's understanding of characters; their emotions and their situations. It also carries information about people and places. Finally, dialogue can help advance the story, for example when one character describes to another character something which has taken place offstage or in the past. This is sometimes called *narrated action*. In his autobiography called *No Leading Lady* (a reference to the fact that there are no women in *Journey's End*), R.C. Sherriff stressed his attempts to write natural-sounding dialogue. He recalled that he wanted 'to use the words that people spoke in everyday life, words and expressions that I would employ myself' (*No Leading Lady*, 34). This needs qualifying, of course, because real speech – the way we talk in our everyday lives – is often rambling and disorganized. In a play every word has to count because space and time are limited.

The rest of this section contains a short summary of *Journey's End* intended as a reference guide. It cannot tell you everything you need to know about the text, not least because, as we have noted, a play is comprised of different ingredients which work together to tell the story.

Things to do

As you read each scene of the play, you need to pay attention to what happens between the characters, but you also need to imagine yourself as a member of the audience *looking* at the scene. What do you see? What do the characters do? Becoming aware of how this happens will help you discuss more confidently what the scene contributes to the meaning of the play as a whole.

Overview

Act one

Place: A dugout in the British trenches at St Quentin in Picardy, northern France
Time: Monday 18 March 1918, evening

The play begins *in medias res* (Latin: *in the middle of things*) with the relief of this section of the Front Line by Captain Dennis Stanhope's Company. Lieutenant Osborne arrives first to take over from Hardy, the ineffectual captain of the outgoing company. Sherriff quickly establishes the strange atmosphere of this part of the trenches – jolly but tense. Much of this section is *expository* – establishing characters, mood, relationships, letting the audience know what has happened previously, and what is going to happen, notably 'the big German attack' (10).[2] A 'tattered map' is produced and the audience learns that the men are responsible for 'about two hundred yards of front line.' They are also close to the Germans whom they can hear at night (11).

The opening exchange also conveys the sense of the trenches as a place of gossip and rumour. Through this, Sherriff builds up the audience's expectations of what young Captain Stanhope will be like. The audience learns that Stanhope, described as 'a boy', is '[d]rinking like a fish, as usual' but that his reputation for bravery and efficiency is unaffected (12–13). However, they learn, too, that he is under severe mental strain. Hardy tells of how, when last on leave, 'all of a sudden he jumped up and knocked all the glasses off the table! Lost control of himself; and then he – sort of – came to – and cried' (13).

The incompetent Hardy is anxious to get away before Stanhope has an opportunity to reprimand him about the poor state of the trenches. Hardy leaves and Mason, a cockney soldier servant acting as cook, arrives to prepare supper. Mason then exits and Lieutenant James Raleigh comes down the dugout steps. He is excited and although this is his first time in the trenches he is feeling lucky. Stanhope was his hero at school and, thanks to some string-pulling, he has secured a place in Stanhope's Company. The audience learns of a further connection between the two men, that there is, or has been, a romantic relationship between Stanhope and Raleigh's sister (who is never seen). Very often in a first scene a problem or *complication* develops which looks as if it is going to disrupt

---

[2] R.C. Sherriff, *Journey's End* (1929) (Penguin Modern Classics, 2000). All subsequent references are to this edition of the play.

the characters' lives. The war is one problem, of course, but Raleigh's arrival is another. The order and sense of routine which Stanhope has established is going to be disturbed.

Captain Stanhope and Lieutenant Trotter arrive. Stanhope, who is twenty-one but seems much older, stares at Raleigh as though he cannot believe it. He treats the new arrival in an unfriendly way including the question, 'How did you – get here?' (23). He is suspicious about how Raleigh has turned up in his trench and states sarcastically that it is, 'Rather a coincidence' (23). This initial encounter sets up one of the main tensions between two of the play's characters and the audience cannot help but notice it.

Mason then serves dinner – to the delight of Trotter who is obsessed with food. However, even he is annoyed by the absence of pepper intended as a 'disinfectant' for the strange yellow soup they are served. 'I mean – after all – war's bad enough *with* pepper – (*noisy sip*) – but war without pepper – it's – bloody awful!' (25). It is important to note the men's concern with apparently trivial things not least because this is a recurrent detail. It contributes to (a) the sense that Sherriff is showing things as they were and (b) the strategies the men cling onto to retain a sense of normality. Meal-times round the table are an important feature of the play. They offer a break in the action but are also a mark of civilized values being continued even in the middle of a war zone. Eating together is a form of communion, of people coming together.

Lieutenant Hibbert comes down the stairs after guard duty. He refuses supper saying he is suffering from what he calls 'beastly neuralgia' and withdraws to his dugout (28). Stanhope is scathing and unsympathetic. Hibbert is described as, 'Another little worm trying to wriggle home' (29). Stanhope begins to drink whisky, a substance he uses as a form of anaesthetic. He confides in Osborne about his feelings concerning Raleigh's arrival. In particular, he is worried that Raleigh will write to his sister and tell her about how Stanhope is faring. Accordingly he decides to censor all of Raleigh's letters. Stanhope is now drunk and Osborne puts him to bed.

Act two, scene one

Place: The dugout
Time: Early Tuesday morning

The scene opens with another meal. Trotter is attacking his breakfast bacon which seems to be mostly fat, the lean bits of meat having shrunk in cooking, according to Mason. The audience is also shown a deeper side of Trotter when he discusses his love for his garden back home. He cheerfully finishes his breakfast, expresses his hope for a hot summer, bids Osborne 'Cheero!' (40) and goes off to relieve Stanhope from guard duty.

After offering some back story relating to Trotter, Sherriff does the same for Osborne who tells Raleigh about his pre-war life. He used to be a teacher and once played rugby for England. In an example of Sherriff's use of understatement, Osborne tells Raleigh about the time when a German officer permitted the British troops to rescue a wounded man from the battlefield. Osborne remarks that the following day they 'blew each other's trenches to blazes'. Raleigh observes that 'It all seems rather – *silly*, doesn't it?', a comment on the war as a whole perhaps (42). He then asks Osborne about the process for sending a letter back home. The mention of the letter acts as reminder of the threat made by Stanhope the previous evening. It signals that a clash between the two men is imminent.

Stanhope enters and explains his plans to secure his section's defences. Osborne picks up on Stanhope's strange attitude to the new arrival. Osborne is the only member of the company who dares tackle him. When Raleigh enters Stanhope tells him to leave his letter unsealed because he, as commanding officer, needs to censor it. Raleigh is taken aback and replies that he will not send the letter after all. Both men are angry but eventually Raleigh hands over the letter. Stanhope cannot bring himself to read it and gives it to Osborne who reads part of it out loud. Contrary to expectation, it is a glowing account of Stanhope.

Act two, scene two

Place: The dugout
Time: Tuesday afternoon

Stanhope discusses the Company's situation with the Sergeant Major – one of the few non-officers to appear in the play. Via this discussion, the audience is reminded again that the Company is facing a German onslaught and there is little prospect of them emerging alive. Since preparations must be made Stanhope calmly orders the strengthening of the wire at the front line and the wiring of the communication trenches so that the men can defend their position to the end. The Sergeant Major shares Stanhope's calm demeanour, making the note: 'Thursday morning. Very good, sir' (50). The exchange between the two men helps illustrate the respect in which Stanhope is held by his Sergeant, a professional soldier.

The Colonel enters with orders for a dangerous raid devised by the Company Commanders at headquarters behind the Front line. The idea is to capture a 'Boche' [German] soldier to get information about the forthcoming enemy attack. Here Sherriff makes one of a number of potentially subversive points about the helplessness of soldiers at the Front – they are at the mercy of men on their own side; they are like the earwigs which Captain Hardy discussed racing against each other in Act One.[3] Realizing that the raid is a stupid and very risky idea, Stanhope thus volunteers to lead it but the Colonel orders that Osborne and Raleigh go instead.

Stanhope's next challenge is to deal with Lieutenant Hibbert whom he believes is malingering. In the play's most melodramatic moment Stanhope threatens Hibbert with a

---

[3] The theory that the soldiers were at the mercy of incompetent military leaders on their own side was later popularized in the 1960s in best-selling history books such as Alan Clark's *The Donkeys* (1961) which attacked upper class generals for staying away from the trenches. The BBC comedy series *Blackadder Goes Forth* (1989) also helped encourage this idea. The theory is still much discussed.

revolver: 'You either stay here and try to be a man – or you try to get out of that door – to desert. If you do that, there's going to be an accident. . . . I'm fiddling with my revolver, d'you see? – cleaning it – and it's going off by accident. It often happens out here. It's going off and it's going to shoot you between the eyes' (56). But in a surprising twist, Stanhope also confides to Hibbert, and by extension, to the audience – who now know more about him than the other characters – that he feels the same fear: 'We *all* feel like you do sometimes. . . . I hate and loathe it all. Sometimes I feel I could just lie down on this bed and pretend I was paralysed . . . and just lie there till I died' (57). After this conversation, Stanhope seems to succeed in bringing Hibbert back on-side but at the cost of revealing his own vulnerability.

The scene ends with Osborne, Trotter and Raleigh finding out about the forthcoming raid. Trotter calls it 'damn ridiculous' (62). Raleigh, in contrast, describes it as 'frightfully exciting' (64). Osborne seems to have a sense of apprehension although he maintains a calm exterior.

Act three, scene one

Place: The dugout
Time: Wednesday, late afternoon

It is time for the raid. The Colonel reveals further details of the logistics to Stanhope, his words reinforcing how dangerous it promises to be. The ineptitude and callousness of high command is thus flagged up again. Osborne asks Stanhope to take care of a watch and wedding-ring and pass them onto his wife in the event of his death. The two men say an awkward farewell. Osborne and Raleigh get ready to lead the attack. Raleigh wants to talk about the raid but Osborne tries to deflect the subject onto other topics notably the novel *Alice in Wonderland* and a shared love for the English countryside. Mason wishes the two men good luck and they leave to the sounds of explosions and smoke bombs.

The raid takes place off-stage. A young German soldier is captured brought into the dugout. Significantly, the sobbing boy is nothing like the brutal beast of popular imagination. The Colonel judges the raid a success but it has been at the cost of Osborne's life and of six other men. Raleigh survives but is in a state of shock. Stanhope, barely able to control his anger at the events which have taken place, reprimands Raleigh for daring to sit on Osborne's bed.

Act three, scene two

Place: The dugout
Time: Wednesday, late evening

It is the same day as the raid and the last evening before the expected German attack. The remaining officers, apart from Raleigh, are shown drinking champagne. Despite the cheery atmosphere they and the audience know that they can expect Osborne's fate. Hibbert gets drunk and boasts about his success with women and produces some pornographic postcards, but he irritates Stanhope who orders him to bed. The men's discussions about women ('tarts') can be read as part of a general misogyny existing within the play itself and certainly the play's interest in male psychology is revealed in the pronouncements made by Hibbert and Stanhope, the play's self-appointed experts on what women 'are' (77–8).

Raleigh appears after guard duty and is questioned by Stanhope about why he did not come to dinner with his fellow offices and ate with the soldiers instead. Raleigh questions how anyone can callously drink and smoke cigars with Osborne lying dead outside. Stanhope flies into a rage. No-one will miss Osborne more than he: 'The one man I could trust – my best friend – the one man I could talk to as man to man – who understood everything – and you think I don't care –' (85). Raleigh's naivety has made him incapable of comprehending but he – along with the audience, if they don't know already, is finally forced to a realization why Stanhope drinks: 'To forget you little fool – to forget! D'you understand? To forget! You think there's no limit to what a man can bear?' (85). At the end of the scene Stanhope appears to have broken down irrevocably. Raleigh leaves. Stanhope is alone as the gunfire sounds outside.

Act three, scene three

Place: The dugout
Time: Approaching dawn, Thursday morning

It is the day of the big attack. Stanhope appears his 'normal' self again. The men follow their usual routines. Trotter is discovered shaving and cracking jokes. He exits cheerfully. Raleigh follows him. Hibbert who is accused of hanging back and 'wasting as much time as you can' (90) is sent out with Mason who has completed his final job of providing the men with sandwiches.

Reports from the trenches suggest that the fighting is going badly. Corporal Ross (unseen) has been hit. Raleigh is carried down by the Sergeant, wounded in the back. Stanhope tries to comfort him but Raleigh, who at first appears not to know how seriously his injuries are, dies. The noise of the shelling gets louder. A messenger appears bringing a message from Trotter asking for Stanhope who goes up the steps to assume yet again the roles of captain and leader. The stage goes dark as an explosion causes the dugout to cave in. The audience is left with only *'the dull rattle of machine-guns and the fevered spatter of rifle fire'* (95).

Contexts

Production history

1927   The play (originally intended as a novel) is drafted for the Kingston-upon-Thames Rowing Club, which regularly stages Sherriff's plays to raise funds. Sherriff encourages the idea that the play is based on real-life situations. 'The ... characters walked in without invitation. I had known them all so well in the trenches ... I was writing about something real, about men I had lived with' (*No Leading Lady*, 35–6). Originally planning to call the play *Suspense* and then *Waiting*, Sherriff finally decides on *Journey's End* and is encouraged by the rowing club to send the play to London theatrical agents (who reject it).

1928   One firm of agents, Curtis Brown, is impressed and sends the play to Geoffrey Dearmer of the Incorporated Stage Society, a prestigious private theatre club. On the advice of playwright George Bernard Shaw, who describes *Journey's End* as 'interesting' as 'a "slice of life" – horribly abnormal life', Dearmer agrees to stage it (*No Leading Lady*, 45). The Stage Society pay Sherriff £15.00 for two performances. *Journey's End* opens on Sunday 9 December at the Apollo Theatre in London. It is directed by James Whale. Stanhope is played by up-and-coming actor, Laurence Olivier. Reviews are positive. *The Stage* calls it 'a vivid and thrilling picture of "the real thing"' with 'commendable freedom from theatrical exaggeration, effective use of well-chosen detail ... acute sense of character and of the stimulating or nerve-wracking influence of a front-line environment' (13 December 1928, 24). This will be a frequent response over the next 100 years.

1929   Despite good reviews no-one is willing to stage the play commercially until actor-turned producer, Maurice Browne, raises enough money. The play re-opens at the Savoy Theatre on 21 January. It runs until 1 June before transferring to another West End theatre, The Prince of Wales, where it runs until 7 June 1930. There are 594 performances in total. A production of the play with British actors also opens in New York, at the Henry Miller Theatre on Broadway, on 22 March. Despite first-night audiences claiming not to understand the British accents, it runs for 485 performances. In the following years the play is performed in twenty-one European countries and translated into other languages including Afrikaans, Japanese and Hindustani. A version opens in the German capital, Berlin, in August

1929 The play is turned into a novel, co-written by R.C. Sherriff with Vernon Bartlett. The novel provides more detail about the characters and their lives before the war.

1929 The play is broadcast on BBC radio on 11 November (Armistice Day). Listeners are advised to listen in the dark so as to be better able to imagine themselves in the dugout.

1930 A film version directed by James Whale for Gainsborough Films opens in Britain on 14 April. Despite being made in Hollywood, it is praised for raising the prestige of British films worldwide.

1934 *Journey's End* is revived at London's Criterion Theatre in December.

1939 The play is revived in New York on 18 September (the start of the Second World War in Britain) but seems out of date. A writer for *Newsweek* sneeringly calls it 'Appeasement Drama', i.e. liable to encourage a mood of defeatism (2 October 1939). The play closes after sixteen performances.

1950 *Journey's End* is revived briefly at the Westminster Theatre in London but does not attract much interest.

1972 The play receives its first major London revival (directed by Eric Thompson) at the Mermaid Theatre. It is well-received and transfers into the Cambridge Theatre in the West End. Peter Egan plays Stanhope. R.C. Sherriff is not consulted about the production. The notorious Vietnam War is happening and the play strikes a chord with peace protestors. However, in the *New Statesman*, the critic, Benedict Nightingale, questions whether the play is really fashionably anti-war as people are saying. He argues that to make this claim is 'to do so without the consent of the author', i.e. Sherriff (26 May 1972).

1976   The film *Aces High*, directed by Jack Gold, and starring Malcolm McDowell in the Stanhope role is released. It retains *Journey's End*'s First World War setting but transposes the action of the play to the Royal Flying Corps – the earlier incarnation of the Royal Air Force.

1988   Seventy years after its first performance the play is revived at London's Whitehall Theatre, directed by Justine Greene, with Jason Connery, famous as TV's Robin Hood, as a dashing Stanhope. In this production, Greene tries to suggest how 'the emotional impact of the play depends on you knowing that it's all inevitable', that the characters will all die (*The Times*, 19 April 1998). Meanwhile, the BBC release a TV version, directed by Michael Simpson, with Jeremy Northam as Stanhope.[4]

1998   A revival of the play at the King's Head Theatre, directed by David Evans Rees with Samuel West as Stanhope, gains much of its impact from the small size of the theatre. 'One is pretty much incarcerated with the men', wrote theatre critic, Sarah Hemming, and she suggested that the play had lost none its power: '80 years on, the raw pity of war strikes us as if new' (*Financial Times*, 15 January 1998).

---

[4] This adaptation, which is largely faithful to the play script, can still be found on You-Tube: https://www.youtube.com/watch?v=y98QdRmLfbQ

2000   *Journey's End* is chosen by the Royal National
             Theatre as one of the 100 Significant Plays of the
             Twentieth Century (ranked 34= with George
             Bernard Shaw's *St Joan*).

2002–11   The play continues to be widely produced in
             amateur and professional contexts. Productions
             include those at the Courtyard Theatre, London
             (2002, directed by Richard Janes) and at the
             Comedy Theatre, London (2004, directed by David
             Grindley), with Geoffrey Streatfield as Stanhope.
             This later revival wins a TONY award in New
             York. The production is revived at the Duke of
             York's Theatre, London, in 2011 prior to a
             nationwide tour. It is directed once again by
             Grindley who, in interviews, argued that the play is
             not an anti-war play because 'the characters feel
             what they are doing is important' (*Sunday Express*,
             17 July 2011).

2014   The Centenary of the outbreak of the First World
             War in August (to 2018) sees more productions
             including one at the Watermill Theatre, Newbury
             (2014). According to critic Giles Woodforde,
             director Paul Hart and actor William Postlewaite
             'make [it] plain that Stanhope is a multi-layered
             character, not just another upper-crust drunk'
             (*Oxford Times*, 25 September 2014). There are
             rumours of a new film based on the play, and starring
             Benedict Cumberbatch and/or Tom Hiddleston.

Things to do

R.C. Sherriff originally planned to call his play *Suspense* and then *Waiting* but dropped these ideas in favour of *Journey's End*. Would you choose one of the earlier titles over the final choice? Why?

Time of writing

Journey's End is about the First World War (1914–1918) but was written ten years after the war ended. The play is thus an example of how the war continued to hold a prominent place in the British cultural landscape of the 1920s. The reasons for this prominence are not difficult to understand. The war was, as Angela Smith notes, a 'cataclysmic conflict', very different from previous conflicts. 'Of the 5,215,162 men who served in the army, 44.4 per cent had been killed or wounded. Very few families escaped unscathed' (*The Second Battlefield*, 2). It was also, as George Parfitt notes, 'a mass war' which 'tested established ways of fighting and new ways of killing'. 'It tested the morale of volunteers and conscripts, the endurance of versatility of women. It went on for a long time and over vast tracts of land' (*Fiction of the First World War*, 2)

When the fighting ended in 1918, there was a widespread sense that a whole generation of young men had been lost. Many never had the chance to fulfil their potential and the playwright J.B. Priestly expressed the views of many when he wrote that 'nobody, nothing will shift me from the belief, which I shall take to the grave, that the generation to which I belong, destroyed between 1914 and 1918 was a great generation, marvellous in its promise' (*Margin Released*, 231). Even those men who seemed physically well, and able to return to family life, were much affected for years afterwards. Shell shock – a term applied to mental breakdown due to the stress of combat – accounted for almost 40 per cent of British casualties. By 1918, hospitals were tending 65,000 shell-shocked patients; 2.5 million others were in receipt of a pension of some other physical disability. Men who had left as celebrated examples of upright British manhood appeared shadows of their former selves.

Britain dealt with the aftermath of the war in a variety of ways. In 1918, work began not only on building 'a land fit for heroes' (to coin Prime Minister David Lloyd George's 1919 electioneering slogan), but of commemorating the dead and of trying to come to terms with the unprecedented slaughter that had taken place. War memorials were erected in towns and villages all over the country and remain with us as very visible symbols of remembrance. The first national 'two-minute silence' was held on 11 November 1919. In 1919, Sir Percy Fitzpatrick argued that such a silence would remind the nation 'of the greater things we hold in common' and the ceremony is still used as a moment of national and international unity (quoted in Adrian Gregory, *Silence of Memory*, 9). We might ask whether Sherriff is attempting a similar memorial to the nation's soldiers in *Journey's End*?

Although Britain and her allies had won the war many people found it difficult to celebrate. The war gradually began to be represented in terms of human suffering and waste, together with the damage caused and the lives wrecked. While it is difficult to pin-point the exact moment at which attitudes began to change, historian Gary Sheffield suggests that it was in 1928 that 'the dam finally burst' on a decade of silent grief (*Forgotten Victory*, 8). This was the year that, in addition to *Journey's End*, saw the publication of *Memoirs of a Fox-hunting Man* by Siegfried Sassoon and *Undertones of War* by Edmund Blunden. They were followed by several more including Robert Graves' *Goodbye to All that* (1929), and Vera Brittain's *A Testament of Youth* (1933). These recollections seemed to offer proof – if proof were needed – of the truth of J.B. Priestly's idea of the 'lost generation'. As writings, they emerged alongside First World War trench poetry by Sassoon, Wilfred Owen, Rupert Brooke and Isaac Rosenberg as the means by which the conflict could be understood on an individual level but also mythologized and given a distinctive imagery which survives to this day: mud, trenches, rats, gas attacks, horrific injuries, death.

Not everyone approved of this kind of war writing. It was seen as unduly depressing but also as disloyal and inaccurate. 'Volume after volume has appeared lately dealing with the War as the experience of individuals and exhibiting it as a more or less unredeemed record of futility and horrors' noted *The*

Times newspaper (7 February 1930, 20). The paper also disliked the focus on one-sided, individual stories and not the 'bigger picture'. In fact, creating the bigger picture was hard to do. Most people had only 'fragments' of knowledge about the war, 'paragraphs – a page perhaps: but no more', to quote the novelist Virginia Woolf. She suggested that her generation were too close to what had happened; they could only get a partial view: 'a glimpse' (*Letters of Virginia Woolf,* 598). Woolf's comments embody something of what the group of writers who became known as 'Modernists' would try to do with their writing, but they also suggest what R.C. Sherriff (not a Modernist) tries to do in *Journey's End*. He does not attempt to show the whole war but rather the experience of a few men at a particular location over a short space of time. For those trying to write about the war both during and afterwards, the full scale of what had happened was hard to grasp, let alone come to terms with, but it *was* possible to describe bits of it.

Post-war theatre

One of the ways in which we can start to understand *Journey's End*, then, is to discuss the play alongside other reappraisals of the war that emerged in the 1920s. This re-visioning also involved the theatre. The theatre of the 1920s is often associated with musicals such as *Chu Chin Chow* (1916–1921) and *No No Nanette* (1925–1926), which were escapist, with catchy tunes and colourful costumes, and also with the sophisticated drawing-room comedies of Noel Coward and Frederick Lonsdale. Nonetheless there *was* an appetite for serious drama. *Journey's End* was just one of several post-war plays which tried to suggest what the conflict had been like for those who fought and its impact on those who had lost loved ones. These plays included: Allan Monkhouse, *The Conquering Hero* (1923); Harry Wall, *Havoc* (1924); Hubert Griffith, *Tunnel Trench* (1924); J.R. Ackerley, *The Prisoners of War* (1925);

Reginald Berkeley, *The White Chateau* (1927); Sean O'Casey, *The Silver Tassie* (1928); Patrick McGill, *Suspense* (1930); and Somerset Maugham, *For Services Rendered* (1932).

George Bernard Shaw, a very distinguished dramatist and critic with some very firm ideas about what made a 'good' play, was one of the people who was asked to read *Journey's End* when it was submitted to the Incorporated Stage Society in 1928. The extract below is his verdict. He starts off by talking about war plays in general then moves on to *Journey's End* and its author more particularly.

Things to do

As you read, take note of what Shaw likes and doesn't like about the play. Do you agree with him? Why does he refer to it as likely to become 'the newspaper of the day before yesterday', i.e. quickly forgotten about?

This play is, properly speaking, a document, not a drama. The war produced several of them. They require a good descriptive reporter with the knack of dialogue. They are accounts of catastrophes, and sketches of trench life, useful as correctives to the romantic conceptions of war and they are usually good of their kind because all those who cannot do them well do not do them at all.

They seem to be useless as dramatist's credentials. The best of them cannot prove that the writer could produce a comedy or tragedy with ordinary materials. Having read this *Journey's End*, and found it as interesting as any other vivid description of a horrible experience, I could give the author a testimonial as a journalist; but I am completely in the dark ... concerning his qualification [as]. . . a playwright. . . .

As a 'slice of life' – horribly abnormal life – I should say let it be performed by all means, even at the disadvantage of being the newspaper of the day before yesterday. But if I am asked to express an opinion as to whether the author could make his living as a playwright, I can only say that I don't know. I can neither encourage nor discourage him.

Quoted in SHERRIFF, *No Leading Lady*, 45

Commentary

One impression we get is, first, that Shaw is dismissive about the long-lasting value of this kind of play; note his phrase 'the newspaper of the day before yesterday'. He means that it will soon be out of date. Secondly, he does not think Sherriff has potential as a dramatist. The value of the play, as Shaw sees it, lies in its use of apparently realistic detail and the way in which it offers audiences a snapshot of trench life – he uses the phrase 'slice of life'. Shaw also uses the phrase 'horribly abnormal life.' On one hand this is recognition that the play *is* dealing with serious subject matter, namely the horrors of the war. On the other hand, Shaw seems to be wondering whether a commercial producer would want to put this play on. This is because in the commercialized theatre of the 1920s producers were often reluctant to invest money in plays about the war. Many believed that the public wanted to forget horrible war-time time experiences when they went out to be entertained.

The popular notion of the theatre as a space for 'a good night out' was one of the challenges Sherriff faced in getting his play produced. 'War plays are supposed be unpopular' noted the *Daily News* (22 January 1929, 6). When *Journey's End* opened at the Savoy Theatre on 21 January 1929 many critics made the same point. They could not believe what they were seeing. This is James Challoner writing in the magazine *The Bystander*:

For this is a war play – stark war in the trenches – and the general opinion is that . . . the ordinary commercial manager, had he read the first ten pages, would doubtless have thrown the script down in disgust. 'No one wants war plays' he would have muttered, and then turned with happy anticipation to some libidinous French farce translated into American. The commercial manager could hardly be blamed for since 1918 we have seen many plays dealing with realities of war, but few have possessed popular appeal (6 February 1929, 262).

It is no surprise that R.C. Sherriff was initially unsuccessful in getting his play staged. 'Every management in London had turned the play down,' he recalled later. 'They asked, how can I put on a play with no leading lady?' (*No Leading Lady,* 43). Eventually he approached the Incorporated Stage Society, a private theatre society which staged one-off showings. They presented the play on 9 and 10 December 1928 at the Apollo Theatre in London with not much hope that anyone would be interested. However, the reaction was mostly positive not least from the country's most influential theatre critic, James Agate, who devoted most of his weekly BBC radio broadcast to praising the play: 'I have never been so deeply moved, so enthralled, so exalted' he told his listeners (quoted in Curtis, *James Whale*, 63).

The big break came when an inexperienced producer, Maurice Browne, decided that he wanted to put the play on in a commercial theatre. He managed to get people to invest in it, notably Dorothy Elmhirst, the daughter of American millionaire William Collins Whitney. She and her husband were interested in the international peace movements which had sprung up in the 1920s. They seem to have been persuaded to read *Journey's End* as a play which was anti-war in its message. When the play re-opened on 21 January 1929 it proved a hit, running for 594 performances. 'All roads lead to *Journey's End*' was the advertising slogan printed on the side of buses. The author Hugh Walpole described being drawn into the events on stage. Convinced of their 'reality' he forgot he was in a theatre at all and left at the end of the evening 'ennobled and simplified by a superb experience' (quoted in Curtis, *James Whale*, 70). He felt a better, more thoughtful person, for having seen it. As will be seen in the section 'Critical reception', Walpole's response is an example of how, in 1929, *Journey's End* appealed to people on different levels. For some it opened their eyes to the experiences of the trenches; for others it took them back there. Others saw it as a celebration of heroism, and as a refreshing change to the trivial musicals and silly comedies found in other theatres.

Things to do

1 Choose one of the following poems, all of which are widely available on the web: Siegfried Sassoon, 'The General', Wilfred Owen 'Anthem for Doomed Youth', Wilfred Owen, 'Arms and the Boy'. Consider how these poets represent the experience of war. Positively? Negatively? Owen's poems were written during the war but were published posthumously in 1920 so are part of the body of literary work which helped change people's perceptions in that decade. How does R.C. Sherriff's attitude to the war-time experience differ?

2 One point made by several critics in 1929 was that Sherriff does seem to draw on a familiar set of images for representing the Front line which had emerged. A writer for the *Saturday Review* described him as 'weaving together' some of the images of 'suffering and sensation' which had become familiar (26 January 1929, 107). A good starting point for some of these images is poetry again. Read Isaac Rosenberg's poem 'Break of Day in the Trenches' (1916). Does Sherriff make use of use any of the same ideas?

Key historical contexts within the play

Journey's End belongs to the genre of the 'history play'. It was written in 1928 but is set in 1918, the fourth year of the First World War – or the 'Great War', as it was termed at the time.[5] As serving soldiers, the war affects the characters at every moment. It is, after all, why they are in the dugout in the first place.

Britain declared war on Germany on the evening of 4 August 1914 – ostensibly because of her obligation to uphold Belgian neutrality. The principal fighting in Europe took place in northern and eastern France and western Russia across muddy patches of ground ('No Man's Land'). The events depicted in *Journey's End* take place on the battlefront in France known to the British as 'the Western Front' (originating from the German label '*die Westfront*' as opposed to the German armies fighting Russia on Germany's 'Eastern Front'). The Front stretched for hundreds of miles, from Ypres in western Belgium down to Nancy in south-eastern France. There were long periods where the battlefront hardly moved and stalemate set in.

This new war bore little resemblance to earlier ideas of warfare. Cavalry charges using horses were quickly abandoned and combatants were faced with new modern weapons: exploding shells, machine guns, tanks, poison gas, aeroplanes, submarines and torpedoes. The numbers of men dying, either on the battlefields or from their injuries was huge: 740,000 British; 1.4 million French; 1.7 million Russian; 1.8 million German (Howard, *The First World War*, 122). The Somme offensive launched by Britain and France in July 1916 resulted in the biggest casualty list in a single day's fighting in British history: the British Army suffered 420,000 casualties including nearly 60,000 on the first day alone. At the Third Battle of

---

[5] For further details see the BBC First World War site: http://www.bbc.co.uk/history/0/ww1/; see also the Imperial War Museum: http://www.iwm.org.uk/history/first-world-war

Ypres (1917), which was intended by the British commander Douglas Haig to be a great breakthrough, troops got bogged down in the mud and the British were left with a few additional kilometres of land and some 310,000 casualties. The characters in *Journey's End* all know this. They are acutely aware that they face the prospect of adding their names to the lists of those killed.

Joining the army: a sign of manhood

British recruitment campaigns often drew on the idea that smaller countries like Belgium needed defending from the German bullies, as did the women and children of Britain. One image which became familiar was the recruiting poster (one of many) showing the face of Lord Kitchener, the government Minister for War, with a pointing finger, 'Your King and Country Need You!' For men, responding to Kitchener's call was a test of their manhood – and also their sense of fair play; they could claim to be defending not only their country but civilization itself.

One of the ways in which *Journey's End* engages with wartime attitudes is by drawing attention to these notions of manhood and duty. In Act Two, Scene Two, when orders have been received about the raid, and when Hibbert is trying to get himself sent to hospital, Stanhope makes this point clearly:

If you went – and left Osborne and Trotter and Raleigh and all those men up there to do your work – could you ever look a man straight in the face again – in all your life? (*There is silence again.*) You may be wounded. Then you can go home and feel proud – and if you're killed you – you won't have to stand this hell any more. . . . But you're still alive – with a straight fighting chance of coming through. Take the chance, old chap, and stand in with Osborne and Trotter and Raleigh. Don't you think it worth standing in with men like that? – when you know they feel like you do – in their hearts – and just go on sticking it because they know it's – it's the only thing a decent man can do (58).

In this speech Sherriff reproduces some of the arguments which had been heard in 1914 and after. In the war's first months many men found it difficult to resist this kind of appeal, rushing to the enlistment offices to become part of a 'citizen army' which soon comprised one million men. The pressure on young men to join was often relentless. Some women adopted the hobby of presenting men who were not in uniform with white feathers, a traditional symbol of cowardice. Some historians have argued that this cruel practice was not as widespread as was once believed and many people disapproved of it, thinking the women silly and ignorant. More acceptable was the use of emotional patriotic songs and poems. This is 'Your King and Country Want You' (1914) by Paul Rubens sung regularly in music halls and variety theatres:[6]

We've watched you playing cricket and every kind of game,
At football, golf and polo you men have made your name.
But now your country calls you to play your part in war.
And no matter what befalls you
We shall love you all the more.
So come and join the forces
As your fathers did before.

Oh, we don't want to lose you but we think you ought to go.
For your King and your country both need you so.
We shall want you and miss you
But with all our might and main
We shall cheer you, thank you, bless you
When you come home again

---

[6] See a clip of the song being performed on You-Tube, recreated for the film *Oh What a Lovely War!* https://www.youtube.com/watch?v=RTJXwOs2_bA

The lyrics of this song were designed to appeal to idealistic young men like Dennis Stanhope and James Raleigh who believed that it was their duty to serve their country and also that the fighting would be like a game of cricket with clearly defined rules and ways of behaving. It became very common in 1914 for writers to fall back on familiar images of bullying, cheating foreigners versus upright, sports-loving Englishmen, 'brothers in arms', God-chosen, fighting for democracy. We could also count Jessie Pope's poem 'Who's for the Game' (1916) as another text which uses the image of sport (in this case, football) to evoke a sense of what young men could expect.[7]

Reading these texts with the benefit of hindsight we know now that the war was not the 'awfully big adventure', to quote J.M. Barrie's Peter Pan, of the kind Jessie Pope, Paul Rubens and others promised. Herbert Asquith's poem 'The Volunteer' is another example of the kinds of images used: chivalric knights on horseback.[8] There *was* comradeship and chivalry but there was also very real likelihood of being blown up by a shell or shot by a sniper or gassed, your body never found.

At the Front: the trenches

In wanting to recreate the war experience it is not surprising that R.C. Sherriff chooses as his play's setting the war's most famous symbol: the trench. Trench warfare and the efforts to secure small patches of territory at the cost of thousands of men's lives became a symbol of the military stalemate especially in the years 1915–1917. There were 460 miles of trenches across Europe which became temporary homes to soldiers and there are many accounts and photos of the grim conditions. On 23 November 1915, Winston Churchill wrote from the trenches at Laventie in France describing 'a wild scene. . . .

---

[7] See: http://www.poemhunter.com/poem/who-s-for-the-game/
[8] See also Herbert Asquith, 'The Volunteer': http://www.poemhunter.com/poem/the-volunteer/

Filth and rubbish everywhere, graves built into the defences . . .
troops of enormous rats . . .' (Soames, 116). Trenches needed
to be deep enough for men to stand up without being exposed
to enemy snipers. They were also narrow in width and zig-
zagged, features intended to offer more protection against
shells. Trenches were notorious for being filthy, muddy, wet
with the potential to cause 'trench foot', leading to gangrene
and amputation. However, in some areas they had underground
bunkers – dugouts – another way of protecting soldiers. One
of the reasons *Journey's End* made such an impact in 1929
stemmed from the seeming-accuracy with which the scenery
makers managed to recreate this on stage. This is W.A.
Darlington writing in the *Daily Telegraph:*

> I had not conceived it possible that any play could so exactly
> recall those old memories. As the first act developed I suddenly
> found myself fighting for self-control, and knew that unless I
> could summon up reserve of restraint from somewhere, the
> first interval would display to the light the shocking spectacle
> of a hardboiled drama critic in tears. I reached the end of the
> act safely and my wife, turning to me, asked: 'Was it like
> that?' I gave a couple of horrible gulps and said: 'Exactly like
> that.' She nodded and said, almost to herself, 'I've never really
> known till now' (22 January 1929, 8).

Behind the trenches on the front line there were support
trenches and communication trenches. A good deal of time
was spent by soldiers in keeping the trenches maintained,
including, at night, repairing the barbed wire at the top of the
trench. Going 'over the top' that is, to say, into battle, did not
come very often. Soldiers rotated between time on the front
line and time spent carrying out duties further behind. A lot of
time was spent patrolling (usually at night) and waiting for
orders from high command – something we also see in
Journey's End – and this sometimes brought with it a sense of
powerlessness and a feeling that the high-ranking officers in
charge did not really know the realities of the situation at the

Front – or if they did, they saw little problem in using men as machine-gun fodder if the bigger aims were to be achieved.

1918: the German Spring Offensive

Journey's End is set in March 1918. Sherriff is very specific about this in his listing of the play's three acts. These dates are significant. It was almost four years since war had been declared. In Britain there was a feeling of war-weariness – food was rationed and there was unrest which took the form of industrial strikes. Nor, on the battlefront, was the news good. March 1918 saw a big push by the German forces under the command of General Ludendorff to break through the allies' defences on the Western Front and onto the French ports and the English Channel. The offensive was called the '*Friedenstrum*' or peace offensive because the Germans hoped that the allies would then ask for peace.

It is this offensive which the characters in *Journey's End* are faced with. 'By the way', Hardy tells Osborne, 'you know the big German attack is expected any day now' (p. 10). When the attack finally came on, 21 March 1918 at 4.50am, German guns opened fire. The German troops outnumbered those of Britain and France and they used an assortment of weaponry to drive through the British positions at Amiens. The Germans moved forwards rapidly onwards, helped by fog which hid them.

Over the subsequent weeks the German forces re-captured much of the land that the British had taken in the autumn of 1917. Commander in Chief of the British forces, Douglas Haig, issued an order to all troops: 'With our backs to the wall and believing in the justice of our cause each one of us must fight on to the end. The safety of our homes and the Freedom of mankind alike depend upon the conduct of each one of us at this critical moment.'[9] It does not, of course, take much to

---

[9] Interactive Timeline of the First World War: http://www.schoolshistory.org.uk/gcse/firstworldwar/firstworldwartimeline/1918/april.htm

connect these words with Dennis Stanhope's plans for his own men in *Journey's End* Although Haig's command would later come to be severely discredited, Sherriff does not do so directly and clearly wants us to admire the soldiers' bravery in carrying it out the orders they were given.

Sherriff admitted that he chose March 1918 deliberately. He later described it as 'the most dramatic episode on the Western front' (*No Leading Lady*, 35). Whether Sherriff also wants his audience to question the military decisions is more complicated. In his autobiography, Sherriff did write that in *Journey's End* the audience are supposed to realize early on that these soldiers are 'caught in a trap with no hope of escape'. The play's end was 'inevitable from the moment it was revealed that [they] . . . had moved into the front line on the eve of the great German offensive that overwhelmed every regiment in its way' (*No Leading Lady*, 38).

Things to do

1 Do a search on Google for some of the propaganda posters used by the British government during the First World War. What messages do the posters send out? What shared values do they appeal to in those who view them?

2 Read Herbert Asquith's, 'The Volunteer' (1914). What is the message of this poem? Are there any characters in *Journey's End* who you think might share its vision?

3 Choose a two-page extract from the play. Read it carefully, making a note of any clues that Sherriff gives us about the period in which it is set. Note: these clues may be in the dialogue or the stage directions.

4 Do a Google image search for an image from the Western Front. Choose an image that you think matches a verbal description offered by one of the characters in the play.

5   In pairs pick any item (clothing, weapon, food) used by
    soldiers in the trenches and use the library and the
    internet to research its significance and importance.

6   Do some research into popular war-time music and
    entertainment. You could begin by finding out about
    Zig-zag starring George Robey – something Stanhope
    refers to in Act One, Scene Two (46). What other topical
    references can you find?

Themes

Most pieces of creative writing have a theme: leadership, duty,
friendship, love, cowardice, loyalty, betrayal and so on.
Sometimes assignment questions ask you to hunt down the
theme and look at how characters, events, dialogue or imagery
contribute in pushing a particular theme to the forefront. It
may be that particular characters or relationships are connected
to a specific theme. For example, when Sherriff began planning
Journey's End, his theme, he later wrote, 'was hero worship'
and he had Raleigh and Stanhope in mind (33).

The dominant theme of *Journey's End* could be said to be
the First World War but this is rather vague. More specifically
we could say that the play is about the effects of war on the
individual – every ingredient comes together in support of this.
The audience is asked to study the officers of the company as
they pass in and out of the dugout. Over the course of three
acts, all the men pass up the stairs which leads to the trenches
and their own death.

Masculinity

We have seen how traditional expressions of honour, duty,
chivalry and self-sacrifice were much to the forefront during

the First World War. War traditionally represented an important test of 'manliness' for young men and the years 1914–1918 were no exception. Even when poets such as Wilfred Owen and Siegfried Sassoon shocked readers by describing the misery and horrors of the trenches in their poems, this idea did not disappear but became re-worked around ideas of suffering and self-sacrifice for the greater good. Nor was this idea rejected outright when the war ended despite the disillusionment. Ideals of gentlemanly conduct, manliness and good sportsmanship persisted and are what Sherriff celebrates in *Journey's End*. For instance we are encouraged to contemplate in Stanhope, Osborne and Raleigh an example of the modern, properly English man. They are a familiar types in early twentieth-century adventure romance novels like P.C. Wren's best-seller *Beau Geste* (1924); models of manhood produced by Sherriff's and indeed his generation's continuing fixation with the construction of gendered identities, and by the cult of the 'manly' boy and the 'man's man'.

Recent historians such as Michael Roper have pointed out that it was the 'no-frills' public [i.e. private] schools which were seen as early training grounds for these kinds of ideals. They emphasized personal qualities such as fairness, endurance, toughness. Self-control – not letting your emotions get the better of you – was also prized. This is what Hibbert fails to live up to in *Journey's End*. We see him '*crying without effort to restrain himself*' (57). As Roper points out, according to the public school way of thinking 'nervous complaints [were] seen as failures of manliness' and needed to be cured by toughening up ('Between manliness and masculinity', 348)

At the beginning of the twentieth century it was believed that this kind of training would equip students for roles in any profession but particularly for service in the British Empire, as it then was, or in the armed forces where war was 'a test of character'. Roper offers a real-life example from 1914 of one young soldier, Lyndall Urwick, who was genuinely anxious about whether he could live up to the popular image of the soldier-hero. In a letter he told his mother: 'All my ideals,

England is fighting for. That I may not disgrace her is my constant prayer' (48). His fears sound eerily similar to those which Sherriff has Stanhope exhibit in *Journey's End* – a worry that he will not live up to the ideals which he has been brought up to follow. One of the things Sherriff does is to show the severe psychological challenges in living up to these kinds of expectations.

Public school was also seen to prepare young men for war because the army had similar structures. This, too, is present in *Journey's End*. Men are forced to obey orders and follow timetables, and the dugout with its (in some ways) immature inhabitants carries with it the aura of the sixth-form common room. Raleigh's letter home reports that Stanhope is 'always up at the front line with the men, cheering them on with jokes, and making them keen about things, like he did the kids at school' (49). Stanhope remains the sports hero and tries to instil a sense of team ethos in Hibbert. 'Shall we see if we can stick it together?' he asks (58). Like a pupil arriving at a new school Raleigh, also, needs to learn how things work. So he is reprimanded by Stanhope (the ex-head boy) for eating with the 'ordinary' soldiers: 'I know you're new to this, but I thought you'd have the common sense to leave the men alone to their meals' (84). Despite the ticking off, there is for Raleigh, something comforting about this. It is like being back at school. Stanhope, however, knows that some things are not the same, not least himself – he *has* changed. He is sure that Raleigh will quickly come to loathe or – worse – pity him.

It is significant that, unlike the work of some of Sherriff's contemporaries – Richard Aldington's angry novel *Death of a Hero* (1929), for example – *Journey's End* does not outwardly appear to question the value of this kind of education or its value in giving structure and meaning to soldiers' experiences. Indeed, rather than criticize it, one of the final exchanges of the play seems to celebrate the whole package. This is the scene where Raleigh (dying) is carried down into the dugout and is ministered to by his old school idol, Stanhope:

Raleigh   Something – hit me in the back – knocked me clean over – sort of – winded me – I'm all right now. (*He tries to rise*)

Stanhope   Steady, old boy. Just lie there quietly for a bit.

Raleigh   I'll be better if I just get up and walk about. It happened once before – I got kicked in just the same place at rugger; it – it soon wore off. It – it just numbs you for a bit. (93)

It is not clear whether Raleigh knows how badly he is injured and is here putting a brave face on it, forcing himself to follow the public school 'code' which he has been taught, or whether he simply expresses himself in the only language he knows. This remains the language which has sport as a point of reference. The same language, of course, works its powers on Stanhope. He is momentarily transported back in time with Raleigh to their schooldays, an innocent period when the war was beyond anything they could comprehend.

It is precisely this kind of scene that has led to Sherriff being seen as 'old-fashioned' – even in 1928. He has often been accused of getting caught up in the romance of the public school product embodied by Raleigh, Stanhope and Osborne. The result is that *Journey's End* is a powerful contributor to the popular tendency whereby, according to Gary Sheffield, 'Upper class ex-public schoolboys have come to symbolise the British army in the First World War' (*Forgotten Victory*, 147). The handsome poet Rupert Brooke (1887–1915), author of 'The Soldier' (1915) is the most celebrated real-life example, his romantic image persisting in soft-focus photographs, as well as verse.[10] *Journey's End*, its detractors argue, likewise celebrates the heroism of the young officers who fought till the death and gives them a similar film-star glamour. '[S]ticking it', as the dashing Dennis Stanhope comments, 'it's the only thing a decent man can do' (58).

---

[10] See: The Rupert Brooke Society http://www.rupertbrooke.com/

On the other hand, it is possible to argue that Sherriff wants his audience to be critical of this public-school value system. It has damaged Stanhope. He thinks that his only worth in the eyes of Raleigh and his fiancée is his heroism in the accepted mould. They both worship him and nothing will stop them 'as long as the hero's a hero' (30). He confesses his fears about not living up to these expectations. His feelings of pride mean that he puts pressure on himself to live up to the ideal but the audience is shown how destructive this ideal is to his mental health.

So: is Sherriff inviting his audience to re-consider or criticize the unrealistic expectations placed on young men and the limited outlook it encourages? He is certainly saying something – via Stanhope – about how personally unpleasant heroes can be.

Hysteria and neurosis

One of the unintended outcomes of the First World War was a greater interest in, and understanding of psychology, the unconscious mind, and the effects of trauma. One famous practitioner of psychoanalysis was Dr W.H. Rivers who, during the war, ran a hospital for 'shell-shocked' soldiers at Craiglockhart near Glasgow. It is estimated that there were 80,000 men diagnosed with this condition during the war.[11] Rivers' patients included Siegfried Sassoon and Wilfred Owen, an episode which forms the basis for Pat Barker's celebrated modern novel *Regeneration* (1991). Rivers is significant from the point of view of the ideas expressed in *Journey's End* because, as Michael Roper points out, 'His treatment of shell-shock victims led him to believe that the condition stemmed . . .

---

[11] The British Pathé News website has some very striking – and moving – film footage of First World War soldiers deemed to be suffering from this condition: http://www.britishpathe.com/workspaces/BritishPathe/shell-shock

from a clash between the instinct to preserve life and the social and military necessity for duty' (349). Part of Rivers' treatment involved trying to get his patients to talk about their experiences much as a therapist might do today, rather than keeping them bottled up. For some patients, it was difficult to do this because they had been trained *not* to talk. The concept of manliness (see above) with which they had been brought up encouraged particular kinds of behaviour and did not include talking about one's fears but acting for the 'greater good' no matter what the personal cost to one's mental health. 'When people are going potty they never talk about it; they keep it to themselves' Osborne tells Stanhope (45).

Journey's End shows how different characters deal with the experience of warfare and the accompanying fear. Trotter draws circles on a chart on the wall so he can tick off each hour of their time at the front. He is mocked by Stanhope for doing so but it is a way of imposing order on things. In addition, whilst Sherriff does not use the medical language of shell-shock to any significant degree the play *is* unusual for its time in showing soldiers as 'hysterical', a mental state doctors previously associated mostly with women. Stanhope, in particular, would be a challenging patient for Dr Rivers at Craiglockhart. It is interesting look at how he conducts himself. He is a man on the verge of a breakdown, or may even have suffered one already. As he admits to Hibbert (another potential patient) he is caught in a bind between experiencing terrible fear but being unable to express it and having to appear to be the kind of idealized man his rank – and society – demands. When wanting to censor Raleigh's letter home he determines to 'Cross out all he says about me'. '[W]e all go west in the big attack and she goes on thinking I'm a fine fellow for ever – and ever – and ever' (33). The fact that he cannot – as Captain – speak about his fear makes his will-power and emotional bravery all the more impressive. His only outlet is Osborne (to a degree), Hibbert (momentarily), and whisky (regularly). It seems apparent that no public school – however rigorous its training – can eliminate a person's fear and Stanhope's effort of will is insufficient on its own. At the same time he publicly expresses contempt for those like Hibbert who cannot do the same.

Hibbert is the other character in whom the theme of neurosis is taken up. He is a character who has always provoked a range of responses. Some critics argue that Hibbert is a representation of R.C. Sherriff himself. As a soldier Sherriff wrote down his own responses to being under attack from shell-fire: 'shell whizzes over . . . feel sick – breathing comes hard, heart beats . . . NERVES'. Later he told his parents that he thought he might be sent home with shell-shock. On another occasion he wrote that he had been off sick because of 'neuralgia', a complaint Hibbert talks about suffering. Rosa Maria Bracco suggests that through Hibbert, Sherriff was perhaps reliving his own fear, something documented in letters to his parents and in his war diary. When Sherriff hoped for a transfer out of the front line, a Commanding Officer accused him of 'trying to get a soft job' (quoted in Braco, *Merchants of Hope*, 156–60). He wrote to his father how 'everyone has a different temperament I know, and I may have got a more imaginative one than suits the necessities of trench life' (*Merchants of Hope*, 163). The confrontation between Hibbert and Stanhope in Act Two, Scene Two, which ends with the latter admitting that he feels 'just as you feel'(57) has thus been read as an attempt by Sherriff to write out his own troubled memories, with play-writing as a form of therapy. By having Stanhope (the most heroic character) say these words, Sherriff tries to excuse his own earlier attempts to deal with fear. When the play premiered, Sherriff was reportedly upset that audiences were not more sympathetic to Hibbert.

Friendship and homosexuality

Journey's End can easily appear an old-fashioned play, especially in the ways the characters express themselves. It has been argued that the most dated exchange in the play is not one which includes expressions such as 'beastly' or 'topping' but a comment made by Osborne. Discussing Raleigh's feelings for Stanhope he observes how: 'There's something deep, rather fine about hero-worship.' The following conversation then occurs:

> **Osborne** He seems to think a lot of you.
>
> **Stanhope** (*Looking up quickly at* **Osborne** *and laughing*) Yes, I'm his hero.
>
> **Osborne** It's quite natural.
>
> **Stanhope** You think so?
>
> **Osborne** Small boys at school generally have their heroes.
>
> **Stanhope** Yes. Small boys at school do.
>
> **Osborne** Often it goes on as long as –
>
> **Stanhope** – as long as the hero's a hero.
>
> **Osborne** It often goes on all through life. . . . You ought to be glad. He's a good-looking youngster. I like him.
>
> **Stanhope** I knew you'd like him. Personality isn't it? (30)

It is this kind of conversation which Samuel Hynes has referred to as 'the hovering note of homosexuality' in the play (*A War Imagined*, 34). None of it is explicit but there are a few small references elsewhere which could perhaps be used to support this observation. For example, after being tucked up in bed by Osborne, Stanhope (jokingly) asks for a kiss Elsewhere Osborne responds angrily to Hardy's criticism of Stanhope saying 'I love that fellow. I'd go to hell with him.' 'Oh, you sweet, sentimental old darling', is Hardy's response (14).

Within the confines of this kind of reading, these details on Sherriff's part can be read as the 'homotextuality', to use Byrne Fone's description, characteristic of so-called gay texts of the period (*A Road to Stonewall*). They raise the issue of how notions of homosexuality are articulated within a culture which does not allow such things to be spoken of openly. We have seen that for the most part, characters in *Journey's End* can only express their feelings indirectly, a comment here, a gesture there. Homosexual relations between men were not decriminalized in England and Wales until 1967 and during the First World War soldiers would have expected to face a court martial if they had been caught engaging in sexual activity. Yet several recent studies have suggested that men did (unsurprisingly) experience some very intense relationships, something captured in Martin Taylor's anthology *Lads: Love Poetry of the Trenches* (1989). Some of them may have been sexual. It has also been suggested that R.C. Sherriff may have been gay (though there is no evidence one way or the other), and that the play somehow reflects this.

The other side of the argument is that this kind of reading of *Journey's End* is anachronistic, that is to say, it is an example of something being slotted into the wrong historical period – just as when we see a character in a film about ancient Rome wearing a wrist watch. Here it can be read as an example of modern critics attempting to impose their own modern interests onto people and characters from an earlier period who would not have explained themselves in this sexualized way. Much perhaps depends on performance and how the relationships are indicated by the actors on stage.

Another approach is simply to argue that what Sherriff is trying to convey is the kind of male-bonds and intense levels of intimacy which the confined conditions and traumatic experiences of the trenches were bound to encourage. Other men who served in the trenches also wrote about these relationships both in diaries and poems. Characters are thus shown being supportive to one another – Osborne helps Stanhope during his darkest moments; Stanhope lets his guard down with Hibbert; and Stanhope comforts the injured Raleigh. The play asks us to celebrate the bonds between the men and the ways in which they look out for each other. Stanhope admits that Osborne is his 'best friend' (85). So we might argue instead that the play is actually a celebration of male friendship and the heights it can achieve.

The power of repression

Osborne   Who's going?

Stanhope   You and Raleigh.
(*Pause*)
Osborne   Oh. (*There is another pause.*) Why Raleigh? (59)

During the course of the play, the audience witnesses how much of the tension created in the play comes from the things that *cannot* be said. A striking thing about Sherriff's writing is the way he avoids melodrama and extreme language (even when the events might seem to call for it). He relies, instead, on silences, which become expressive, and on understatement. The soldiers are 'frightfully annoyed' when their dug out is blasted by a shell. When Osborne describes how a German officer ordered a cease-fire so the British could rescue a wounded comrade, he recalls that next day 'we blew each other's trenches to blazes'. Both he and Raleigh agree that 'It all seems rather – *silly*', one of several low-key comments on the horrors of the war itself (42). When Stanhope says 'Cheero!' to Osborne as the latter sets out on the raid likely to result in his death, Sherriff offers the following stage direction: '*For a second their eyes meet; they laugh.* **Stanhope** *goes slowly up the steps. There is silence in the dugout*' (68). There are no words to express the depth of what they feel but both men understand each other.

Some people might say that this kind of deliberate suppressing of emotion is a recognizably – or stereotypically – British characteristic. 'Making a fuss' and getting upset has traditionally been seen as self-indulgent and not the behaviour of sensible, 'well-brought up' people. Even a working-class character like Mason is seen to share this phlegmatic attitude. Hibbert, of course, struggles to behave like this and is judged harshly by the other characters.

It is also possible that Sherriff is trying to convey a very specific war-time sentiment. One of the popular ideas circulating between 1914 and 1918 was that people could contribute to the country's war effort by 'carrying on' as normal – or at least as far as possible. The catchphrase 'business as usual', generally attributed to David Lloyd George when he was Chancellor of the Exchequer, was also used a good deal. He had coined it in August 1914 in a speech to businessmen as part of a plan to reduce the effect of the war on the economy. People needed to avoid panicking and stay calm. If they followed this advice all would be well. 'Carrying on' came to be championed as patriotic; an opportunity to show a kind of devil-may-care attitude, something which Sherriff's characters seem to have taken up and sometimes display in their interactions with each other.

In terms of stage performance it is also worth thinking about the effect that understatement has on an audience. At the end of the nineteenth century some theatre critics argued that, in terms of acting, understatement was more powerful than overstatement. One such was William Archer who wrote that that 'the actual shedding of tears is not, in itself, particularly effective [on stage], and that we Anglo-Saxons of this generation are perhaps less apt than our ancestors ... to be moved by ... unrestrained weeping'. Instead, he argued that: 'One of the most touching of all phases of activity is the successful repression of tears' (*Masks or Faces?*, 55–6). In the 1920s, the critic and director, J.T. Grein, took Archer's idea further and argued that on stage, as in real life, a much more effective impression was liable to be made 'by restraint' and 'suppression', the actor indicating rather than loudly emphasizing 'the turmoil within' (*The New World of the Theatre*, 152–3).

It is possible to make links here to Sherriff's characterization in *Journey's End* and the downbeat style in which the play is usually performed. The men are at the end of their tether – tormented, scared, tired – Stanhope's hands shake, he downs whisky, he loses his ability to speak clearly – but as British soldiers he and his men can never express fully their feelings; they have to keep them buttoned up and repressed – under a cold exterior in Stanhope's case. This makes the play all the more moving – and tense. Part of the psychological power of the play comes from knowing that the men, particularly Stanhope, might boil over – or break down – any moment.

When they *do* try to express what they feel, as in the case of Hibbert, they have to be silenced and brought back into line.

Is the theme in the title?

A clue to what the play is 'about' is present in its naming: *Journey's End*. It is a quote from William Shakespeare's tragedy *Othello* (written around 1603), a play about a black military hero who is betrayed and brought down by those closest to him. In Act V Othello gives a famous speech of surrender, clutching a dagger, before committing suicide:

> **Othello**   ... But (O vain boast!)
> Who can control his fate? 'tis not so now.
> Be not afraid, though you do see me weapon'd;
> Here is my journey's end, here is my butt,
> And very sea-mark of my utmost sail.
>
> V.II. 259–6

Othello's speech is partly about man's inability to remain master of his own destiny, no matter how bravely he tries. *Journey's End*, we could argue, expresses similar sentiments. The men fight bravely but their fates (and journeys) are beyond their control. Higher powers – most obviously the army's High Command, but also the Christian God – dictate their fate. Like Othello, their deaths can be interpreted as a kind of martyrdom.

Another reading of the title, which need not exclude the first, is that it is a reference to John Bunyan's *The Pilgrim's Progress* (1678). This religious book describing the journey of a man (Christian) from the 'City of Destruction' to seek God in the 'Celestial City' has been extremely influential in the history of British literature. The book's story is an *allegory* (a text in which the characters and plot symbolize other ideas). At the end of *The Pilgrim's Progress*, after a journey full of danger, Christian and his companion, 'Hopeful', arrive at the gates of the City and are led in with much rejoicing. The book's promise of eventual salvation made it well known and much quoted during the First World War, not least because its ending struck a chord with people battered and confused by events. Of course, there is little sense of praise and exultation in Sherriff's *Journey's End*. The life journey for this group of men ends not with the celestial city but the filth of the trenches. However, another reading might be to say that the trenches are only part of their journeys. After death these will continue and they, like Bunyan's Christian, will reach the celestial city (i.e. heaven).

Characters

In 1934, Russell Gregory watching a revival of *Journey's End*, suggested that the only way to enjoy it was 'to forget it is a war play'. 'The fact that it takes place in a dug-out in France is of no more significance than that Alice's adventures took place on the other side of the Looking-Glass.' In this play it was the story of the characters that mattered and it was primarily a work about the tensions between the men (*Saturday Review*, 15 December 1934, 541). Sherriff's own comments seem to bear this out. He wrote that he was interested in his characters' 'relationships with each other' and in his ability to 'weave a pattern' out of them (*No Leading Lady*, 37).

It is true that when we watch any play, film or television drama we expect to be engaged by, or at least interested in, the characters. *Journey's End* is no exception. We see different people *in action* responding to desperate circumstances. We get to learn something about them as a result. It is because of this that we need to pay attention to what the characters are shown to say and do, and also how they behave when faced with a particular choice or decision.

Another aspect of characters worth noting has to do with their function communicating information to the audience. Take Captain Hardy. His long scene with Osborne in Act One is the major piece of *exposition* in the play, the insertion of important background information. Thus we learn about

Hardy himself but Sherriff also uses this opening scene to reveal to the audience the problems being experienced by the British troops, and also Stanhope – and gives hints about his mental state before he appears. Characters also communicate details of offstage happenings, for example, the raid in Act Three. This is a useful technique for the author: *condensation*. It would be impossible to depict all the events of the raid on stage in a convincing way. It would also make a very long (and expensive) play. There would also be the issue of how to show Osborne's death by grenade. This might distress or alarm an audience. Instead, having characters narrating events works on the audience's imagination, they may even be more affected by them than if the author had tried to show them on stage.

In discussing one or more of the characters from a play you need to think about how they are *delivered* to the audience. Walls and Shepherd write of how most characters are 'progressively revealed to us' in the play text, that is, the audience knows them better at the end of the play than at the beginning. This means paying attention to how they are delivered on the page but also how they might be delivered in a stage performance (31). This last point is important because an actor can do a lot to influence character delivery through the gestures he or she uses, the accent he or she adopts, together with the tone of voice used to deliver a line. Norman Page notes how 'in the theatre, simply by being present as an individual with his own physique, costume, movements, facial and vocal qualities . . . the actor endows the role he is playing with his own unique individuality' (*Speech in the English Novel*, 99). The way in which a character is delivered is often out of the author's control no matter how many stage directions he or she includes in the original script.

Finally, the characters represented in a play can tell us a lot about the culture in which the play was written. *Journey's End* was written in 1928 and set in 1918. Most of the characters in the play are thus part of the so-called 'war generation', that is, people born in the last decade of the nineteenth century (1890s). Socially, the play has a narrow range and has been attacked for this; it is not like Shakespeare's *Romeo and Juliet* which includes a Duke and the wealthy, upper class citizens of Verona, but also priests and humble servants. Sherriff does not give us the whole social make-up of the army despite the fact that the war was supposed to be a moment where class barriers began to break down. Instead, the characters are mostly privately-educated, middle-class men (Trotter, Mason and the Sergeant being the three exceptions) and whilst we hear about other ranks ('the men') we never get to hear any of them discussing anything themselves. They do not have much of a voice.

Stanhope

Dennis Stanhope is a striking example of a character gradually revealed to the audience. He is first drawn to the audience's attention *before* he appears on stage. This is via the conversation between Captain Hardy and Lieutenant Osborne which is designed to build up interest and suspense. Hardy comments on Stanhope's mood swings and his reputation for excessive drinking, revealing that he has become an object of curiosity for other soldiers, 'a freak show', a 'hard drinker' whose 'nerves' are 'all to blazes' (12–13). However, the two men also flag up Stanhope's qualities as the 'best company commander we've got'. He has been in the trenches for three years solidly and has not taken the leave to which he is entitled. 'Other men come over here and go home again ill, and young Stanhope goes on sticking it, month in, month out . . . I've seen him on his back all day with trench fever – then on duty all night' (13). He has been decorated for bravery (with the Military Cross) and at the age of twenty-one is already a Captain in command of a Company.

When Stanhope speaks for himself the audience sees that he is a figure of superhuman mental strength but is also vulnerable and isolated. The stage description of his appearance conveys strain: '*Although tanned by months in the open air, there is a pallor under his skin and dark shadows under his eyes*' (22).

Stanhope admits the reason he has not been back to Britain since the battle at Vimy Ridge is partly because he despises the people back home – 'the worms', 'pigs' and 'shirkers' – but also does not want Madge (his fiancée and Raleigh's sister) to see what he has become (32). 'Has he been talking already?' he asks soon after Raleigh's arrival (29). This becomes a nagging fear.

When the play premiered commercially in 1929, one of the objections was the constant reference to Stanhope's reliance on alcohol. Almost every time a new character enters the dugout, they are asked, 'Will you have a drink?' Sherriff is perhaps highlighting the way in which the army authorities believe drink – which there is plenty of – is a remedy for everything. It does seem to work in Stanhope's case – it fuels him to carry on at the same as destroying him – and for the most part does not interfere with his ability to do his job (one of the play's implausibilities perhaps). He is shown to be efficient and maintains the loyalty of those under his command. As the play opens, the audience learns that he is outside 'looking after the relief', a task someone else might be expected to do (17). But drinking is also shown to be affecting his judgement as when he becomes determined to censor Raleigh's letters. He knows that Raleigh has seen him drunk and fears that he has gone down in his estimation. What Raleigh thinks *does* matter to Stanhope – and not just because he thinks he will write home about him. Stanhope's reaction to Raleigh's death conveys the depth of feeling between the two.

The audience also sees that Stanhope is hyper-sensitive. Being sensitive makes him a good leader – a new kind of hero perhaps – because he is able to empathize with his men. However, it also makes him paranoid and vulnerable. Samuel Hynes has written of the emergence in post-war literature of 'the damaged man . . . as a sympathetic figure' (*A War Imagined*, 304). It is possible to see Stanhope as part of this 1920s view which begins to see First World War soldiers as victims.

It is a sign of Stanhope's damaged personality that he seems not to believe in anything – certainly not in victory. 'It's a habit that's grown on me lately – to look right through things' (45).

Nothing apart from alcohol, can comfort him. He has lost his illusions and knows the patriotic values the men think he embodies do not help him. Yet because he despises those who don't fight he has to 'stick it' – despite believing the war to be a horrible error of judgement. He has to remain loyal to his men and pretend that he is well. Perhaps the darkest moment in the play comes when Stanhope reveals that he exists in a kind of waking nightmare in which he feels a closer relationship with the dead than the living. He tells Hibbert: 'Supposing the worst happened – supposing we were knocked right out. Think of the chaps who've gone already. It can't be very lonely there – with all those fellows. Sometimes I think it's lonelier here' (58).

Another point to note is that Stanhope is not necessarily likeable. The confrontation with Hibbert in Act Two, Scene Two and the ways in which Stanhope manipulates the junior officer is gripping but repellent and it gives a clue to Stanhope's mind and how it works. His comment to Hibbert after he pulls the gun on him is: 'Good man, Hibbert. I liked the way you stuck that' (57). It is as if Hibbert has passed a test – or come through a psychological tunnel to a new place where knowing you are going to die brings renewed strength.

Things to do

Go through the text, picking out comments other characters make about Stanhope, positive and negative. What kind of picture of him can you put together from these?

James Raleigh

Osborne 'I hope we're lucky and get a youngster straight from school. They're the kind that do best.' (11)

The stage description of Raleigh describes him as '*healthy looking*'. He has a '*boyish voice*', makes use of schoolboy phrases ('How topping') and is marked by hesitant speech – intended to convey his lack of confidence and experience (16). His lack of knowledge is also that of the audience. As aspects of trench procedure are explained to him, they are explained to us as well.

After Stanhope, Raleigh is probably the most important character. One of his functions is that of the *outsider* whose appearance in the world of the play shakes things up and makes other characters – notably Stanhope – look nervously over their shoulders. He provokes fear in Stanhope. This unease is evident in their awkward reunion (accentuated by the body language): '*Stanhope stares at Raleigh as though dazed. Raleigh takes a step forward, half raises his hand, then lets it drop to his side*' (23). Neither man knows how to behave.

Dramatists sometimes use characters who stand for – or channel – certain qualities and are subsequently seen displaying them in particular situations. Sometimes they can seem cartoonish but often they are there to make the audience think about certain beliefs, attitudes and histories – the histories of the teenagers who volunteered for and were killed in the war, for example. Raleigh is a character who is seen to have a personality but he is also the embodiment of a certain First World War 'type' – the chivalrous young man of the kind celebrated in Herbert Asquith's poem 'The Volunteer' (1914) who joined up with excitement in the hope of serving their country like knights of old. Raleigh is shown as a character who begins hopefully and unsuspectingly, ignorant and excited about trench life and its dangers. 'How topping if we both get the M.C.' he comments before the fateful raid (70).

The First World War is also often described in terms of a shift – from initial enthusiasm to disillusionment, as people began to realize its human cost. Sherriff tries to show something of this journey via Raleigh. One prompt is Osborne's death. Raleigh's reaction shows him in a state of shock: '*walking as though he were asleep*' (76). It seems to be his first experience of death. He sits on Osborne's bed – seen by Stanhope as a gesture which is ill-mannered and callous. But Raleigh is traumatized. He has seen seven comrades killed in return for a very small amount of enemy intelligence. His response seems to be to try to model himself on Stanhope by continuing as normal. The other officers remark that he is 'too keen on his duty'. Even when fatally wounded he says, 'I feel rotten lying here – everybody else – up there' (94). Sherriff is perhaps sowing the seeds of an idea that eventually had he lived, Raleigh would have turned into Stanhope.

The other thing that marks Raleigh is his admiration for Stanhope. From what he says privately to Osborne, we learn that he volunteered to fight because of Stanhope whom he has worshipped – or loved – since school when the older boy was captain of rugby.[12] In one of the play's examples of understatement Osborne prepares Raleigh by telling him 'you mustn't expect to find him – quite the same'. This is due to the war. 'It-it tells on a man – rather badly' (19). Although Raleigh appears guileless, Stanhope treats him as a domestic spy. Yet when Osborne quotes from Raleigh's letter home it becomes clear that Stanhope's fears are misplaced. Raleigh is as admiring of him as he ever was.

Raleigh's symbolic role in the play becomes most obvious with his death. When the play was first produced many people found this last scene intensely moving. One critic, Anthony Bertram, talked of 'human boyishness that is killed like a spring flower trampled upon' (*Fortnightly Review*, April 1930, 578). In this sense Raleigh becomes a memorial to all the millions of young men who were killed in the trenches – 'the lost generation' and the waste of life involved. His death also invites us to consider whether the play's title – *Journey's End* – is a reference to Raleigh. His life is a journey that ends hardly before it has started.

---

[12] Sherriff's novel of *Journey's End* (1930) makes Raleigh's adoration of Stanhope even more explicit.

In terms of the dynamics of the play, it is also worth noting that Raleigh's death is the trigger for the audience to see the real Stanhope who lets his guard down briefly, revealing himself fonder of Raleigh than he has been prepared to show. The play's final exchange between Raleigh and Stanhope allows the audience to recalibrate their feelings for Stanhope – he shows human kindness and we glimpse the person he once was.

Things to do

Using the first person perspective, expand and complete the letter written by Raleigh to his sister which Stanhope wants to censor. Think about how Raleigh might be feeling in relation to his own new experiences and his concerns about Stanhope. Next, write a brief (100-word) commentary, reflecting on your choices of style and content within the letter.

Osborne

'Osborne, *you* ought to be commanding this company', announces Captain Hardy in the first scene (13). Osborne's nickname, 'uncle', signals his maturity (he is in his forties while the others are in their twenties). Age also gives Osborne a different perspective on things. Of his rugby career which impresses Raleigh, he comments, 'It doesn't make much difference out here' (41). He is also a perceptive judge of human nature. He warns Raleigh that he should not expect Stanhope to be the same as he was in England. We also see evidence of his diplomacy when he tries to relieve the tension when Raleigh first appears.

Part of Osborne's role is as a confidential listener – a type of character to whom others reveal things, and by extension, to the audience. Sherriff is not writing a verse drama of the kind we associate with William Shakespeare, so there is no chorus. Nor is *Journey's End* a novel, so there is no narrator. So Sherriff has to use his characters' conversations to get information and explanations across to the audience and several of the scenes with Osborne have this function.

Through these conversations, the audience learns that one of Osborne's characteristics is his loyalty to Stanhope. This is evident at the beginning of the play when Osborne talks to Captain Hardy. Osborne is a patient man and understands – as the other men seem not to – what is happening to Stanhope and why he is worth sticking with: 'He was out here before I joined up. His experience alone makes him worth a dozen people like me' (14). He also becomes protective of Raleigh, and hides from him his own fears about the raid. At the same time his response to the news that he has been picked, 'I see', suggests resignation to his likely fate, i.e. death (60). This is further emphasized when he removes his wedding ring thus severing the bonds with home for the final time. He also reveals a lively intelligence and seems impatient with seemingly unimaginative men like Trotter with whom he has nothing in common – apart from the fact that they share circumstances.

One of the things which emerges is that Osborne is an expert at employing coping strategies. He tries to share one of them with Raleigh:

> **Raleigh** I knew they fired lights. [*Pause*] I didn't expect so many – and to see them so far away.
>
> **Osborne** I know. [*He puffs at his pipe*] There's something rather romantic about it all.
>
> **Raleigh** (*eagerly*): Yes I thought that too.
>
> **Osborne** You must always think of it like that if you can. Think of it all as – as romantic (21).

The men cannot think about death continually – it would drive them to a breakdown. Instead, they try to displace it in every way they can. Like Trotter, Osborne reminisces about his garden at home and talks about the war as if it were a game of rugby. He also reads *Alice in Wonderland*. Trotter cannot understand why a man would read 'a kid's book' but Osborne's liking for it is not just a wish to return to childhood. The book serves as a kind of commentary on the war. The 'topsy turvey' world which Lewis Carroll portrays was often invoked in 1918 to sum up the chaos and confusion which people living through conflict felt they were experiencing. It was Wonderland become reality – nothing seemed to make any sense anymore and everyone was mad!

Osborne's death is reported indirectly. Stanhope tells the Colonel how 'Four men and Raleigh came safely back' (76). It is left to the audience to surmise that Osborne is dead. According to Stanhope (through whose perspective we are told these events), Osborne's death came about because of '[a] hand grenade – while he was waiting for Raleigh' (76). It would have been difficult to show Osborne's death on stage. Rather Sherriff chooses to have Stanhope deliver the information as a way of letting the audience imagine for themselves what has happened. In terms of war casualties, Osborne's death is an example of another man 'lost' (his body is not retrieved). However, Stanhope's reaction to Osborne's death shows that it is much more than this. He relied on the older man to bolster own confidence and sense of self-worth.

Things to do

1 In no more than 300 words and, with reference to events of the play, explain concisely why Osborne's death is such a momentous event for Stanhope?

2 Osborne (and Stanhope) are described as excellent sportsmen. Why might sportsmen be thought to make good soldiers? Do some research into the Sportsman's Battalions which were formed during the war.

Hibbert

From the moment he first appears Hibbert is revealed as someone who complains a lot. Physically he is an unimpressive figure. Stage directions describe him as '*small*', '*slightly built*', '*with a little moustache and a pallid face*', details suggesting weakness (28). When he exits he '*sneaks quietly away*' as though he has something to hide (82). From his first entrance he is also cast as an outsider – someone who is not fully part of the team.

Hibbert is far from being the heroic soldier of popular imagination. He says that he is in pain because of neuralgia but Stanhope is unsympathetic, labelling him a 'worm' and tells Osborne that Hibbert's pain is pretence so that the 'artful little swine' can be sent back to Britain. As he explains: 'No man of mine's going sick before the attack. They're going to take an equal chance – together' (29). These tensions between Stanhope and Hibbert in Act One foreshadow the later confrontation between the two men in Act Two, Scene Two and reveal Stanhope as an officer who asks for total commitment from the men under his command.

The subsequent cut-and-thrust confrontation between the two men is a battle in its own right. It is also an example of how stage dialogue can draw the audience in and make them take a position. Who do we support? The climactic moment of the scene is when, in order to stop Hibbert from – as he sees it – deserting, Stanhope threatens to shoot him with a revolver. Hibbert tries to explain how he feels: 'It's got worse and worse, and now I can't bear it any longer. I'll never go up those steps again – into the line – with the men looking at me – and knowing – I'd rather die here.' [*He is sitting on Stanhope's bed, crying without effort to restrain himself.*] (57). The dashes in these lines are intended to represent broken speech. Stanhope then confesses that he, too, is scared.

Stanhope   I know what you feel, Hibbert. I've known all
along –

Hibbert How *can* you know?
Stanhope Because I feel the same – exactly the same! Every
little noise up there makes me feel – just as you feel. (57)

Because Hibbert is represented fairly unsympathetically most
of the time, the audience is liable to overlook or dismiss
what he says. (This is despite the fact that some of the
things he says match those of Stanhope.) He flags up the
apparent meaninglessness at the centre of the war: 'What does
it matter? It's all so – so beastly – nothing matters?' (58). Yet at
the end of the exchange the characters have reached a new
understanding – as have the audience. They are invited to look
at both characters in a slightly different way.

On the morning of the final raid, Hibbert retains his
composure, although he is accused by Stanhope of 'wasting as
much time as you can' (90). The stage directions indicate that
he exits up the steps *'with a slight smile'* as if he is now resigned
to his fate. Perhaps he recognizes that Stanhope has won their
personal battle (91).

Trotter

Trotter is from a different class background to the other officers.
He is what was known during the war as a 'temporary
gentleman', that is, a soldier who works his way up through the
ranks to gain a commission to become an officer. He is not
public school educated and Sherriff (rather snobbishly we might
think) presents him as a stolid character whose main topic of
conversation is food. His name, 'Trotter' is presumably meant
to suggest a pig! Thus Act Two opens with Mason serving
breakfast and Trotter talks about previous cooks. We see
Trotter's good nature and his apparent contentment with life,
especially if food is involved. Many of his lines involve food:

Trotter What a lovely smell of bacon!
Mason Yes, sir. I reckon there's enough smell of bacon in
'ere to last for dinner.

> **Trotter**   Well, there's nothing like a good fat bacon rasher
> when you're as empty as I am. (36)

Trotter's words 'empty as I am' might be intended to signal his
own hollowness. Certainly he is regarded by the other
characters as too shallow, stupid or unimaginative to be
touched by the horrors of the trenches. Yet he is gradually
revealed to be deeper than first appears. For example, a remark
about a lone bird singing in No Man's Land moves into a
wistful discussion of his garden back home:

> **Trotter**   Funny about that bird. Made me feel quite braced up.
> Sort of made me think about my garden of an evening –
> walking round in me slippers after supper, smoking me pipe.
> **Osborne**   You keen on gardening?
> **Trotter**   Oh, I used to do a bit of an evening. I'ad a decent
> little grass plot in front, with flower-borders – geraniums,
> lobelia, and calceolaria – you know, red, white, and blue.
> Looked rather nice in the summer. (38–9)

Osborne later speaks to Stanhope of his own time in his garden
saying of his last leave how rather than visiting the theatres, 'I
spent all the time in the garden, making a rockery' (46). At
different points in the play the garden becomes a symbol of
Englishness, a version of the Biblical Garden of Eden, a way of
life being fought for: peaceful, green, rural – the complete
opposite of No Man's Land. War-time propaganda posters often
carried pictures of country cottages and green fields and Sherriff
tries to show the hold of these images over these men. The
audience is also reminded just how long Trotter has been serving
in the trenches when he recalls the spring of the previous year
(1917) when a may-tree growing unexpectedly near the trenches
caused panic because its scent was mistaken for poisoned gas
and a gas attack: 'Why, a blinkin' may-tree! All out in bloom,
growing beside the path! We did feel a lot of silly poops – putting
on gas masks because of a damn may-tree!' (39).

Thus while Trotter seems, like Mason, to be devoid of much
imagination or deep feeling, there are several hints that this is

not so. 'Always the same, am I?' he retorts to Stanhope, [*He sighs*] 'Little you know –' (82). The audience is also left with a sense of Trotter's resilience. He is possibly the toughest of the group, conscious of his 'dooty' as he calls it and of sticking with things to the bitter end uncomplainingly. His refusal to be rattled seems to annoy Stanhope (who as we know is *very* rattled) but after Osborne's death he is made second in command, recognition of his reliability.

Things to do

What do you think makes Trotter such an important character in the play? One way of approaching this task is to first consider what the play would lose if his character were cut entirely.

Mason

Mason, the cook, is used in the play to provide moments of comic relief as he pops in and out, breaking up the action. He is not an officer but a working-class soldier, something conveyed through his language, including words like 'sambridges' [sandwiches] and 'lorst'. He feeds the men and could be seen as a mother-substitute, but it is made clear that he also fights alongside them. In the play's final scene he changes clothes and goes back in the trenches with Hibbert whom he treats kindly.

Mason has proved a surprisingly controversial character. In particular, he is seen as further evidence of R.C. Sherriff's snobbery. One of the critics who saw the first production in 1929 found fault in the following way. He wrote: 'Of course an atmosphere of violence begets bad jokes, and though it was admirable in the trenches that anyone should have found anything to laugh at, on stage the comic relief supplied by the cook orderly, the perpetual plum and apple Bairnsfather humour, is painful' ('C.C.', *'Journey's End'*, *New Statesman*, 2 February 1929, 531). The complaint here is that in Mason, Sherriff has given the audience a clichéd, cartoonish character rather than respecting properly the experience of men from the working-class who served in the trenches. The reference to 'Bairnsfather' is to a famous series of war-time cartoons by Captain Bruce Bairnsfather which featured the humorous sayings and adventures of a fat, cynical soldier called 'Old Bill'. If you read the play carefully there are hints that, like Trotter, Mason is more sensitive than he first appears. However, many critics would still argue that Sherriff's representation is based on a stereotype which patronises the working-classes and makes use of the clichéd figure of the comic servant, a dramatic type stretching back to Shakespeare's plays.

Things to do

1 Describe the part played by Mason in the play. Why is he there?

2 Make list of the strategies each character in the dugout adopts in order to cope with the situation?

3 It is the night before the raid. Imagine that you are either one of the officers in the play, Mason the cook, or the Sergeant Major. Write a letter to a member of your family. You are aware that this may be your last letter. Rather than include details that might upset the person receiving the letter, you focus your letter on the acts of comradeship, kindness and self-sacrifice that you have seen among the men you serve with. Use examples from the play to help you.

Captain Hardy

Hardy only appears in Act One. His main function is expository. He is also used to help the audience get a sense of day-to-day trench life. He seems easy-going and thus very different from Stanhope. We see him in cheerful mood and this may be because he knows he is getting out at an opportune moment. The German attack is imminent and Hardy, along with the Colonel, are we assume, the only characters who will survive it. Hardy thinks little of Stanhope and he suggests that Osborne, as the older man, should be in charge.

Sergeant Major

He is an undeveloped character although his loyalty to Stanhope and commitment to the cause are shown. He is a trusted soldier but seems to share Stanhope's cynicism. He is also a device allowing the audience to see Stanhope's other side, i.e. as an organized and accomplished company commander. Sherriff's description of him ('*A huge man, with a heavy black moustache, a fat red face, and massive chin*' (50)) is reminiscent of the war-time cartoon character 'Old Bill' (see the comments on Mason, above).

The Colonel

His function is to show something of the chain of command operating in the army. Through him, we see that Stanhope and the others are simply cogs in the massive war machine. They have little free will and have to obey orders. Reviewing the 1972 revival of *Journey's End*, Benedict Nightingale from the *New Statesman* believed Stanhope created 'the real pathos of the evening' because his 'decency . . . was exploited and abused by the smug, crassly incompetent' military command (26 May 1972). As the play's representative of this command, the Colonel appears sympathetic but does show that he is not really interested in the ordinary soldiers, regarding them as machine-gun fodder. Here Sherriff makes use of a new (controversial) image of military command which emerged after the war as people began to question how it had been run. The Colonel is slightly embarrassed at having to pass on the orders for the raid saying, 'You know quite well I'd give anything to cancel the beastly affair' (67). Nonetheless he expects the raid to be carried out. This is despite Stanhope's sensible arguments to the contrary, not least that the Germans are expecting it and it is certain to cost lives. Afterwards the Colonel appears to have forgotten the human cost, exclaiming, 'It's a feather in our cap, Stanhope' (75). He expects Stanhope to share his satisfaction.

The German prisoner

This young soldier is captured in the raid and brought into the dugout. He only appears briefly but his function is to show that the enemy are not monsters and that he is a very ordinary young man – described as 'a boy' – who is frightened and helpless (74). Perhaps he is a German version of Raleigh? He gives up information about the enemy positions thus allowing the Colonel to declare the mission a success.

Things to do

1   In 1927, the novelist E.M. Forster made a distinction between *flat* and *round* characters. *Flat* characters, who tend to be less prominent in novels and plays, are those who we do not get to know very well – they are always the same. They tend to be distinguished by a single trait or catchphrase and can seem cartoonish. *Round* characters meanwhile, appear more like the people we might encounter in 'real life', possessing a mixture of

features and emotions, and the author tries to suggest a complex personality which gradually emerges over the course of the events. According to Forster flat characters 'are sometimes called types, and sometimes caricatures. In their purest form, they are constructed round a single idea or quality: when there is more than one factor in them, we get the beginning of the curve towards the round.' An advantage of flat characters, argued Forster was 'that they are easily remembered . . . afterwards. They remain in [the] . . . mind as unalterable for the reason that they were not changed by circumstances' (*Aspects of the Novel*, 73–4). We can transfer these ideas to *Journey's End*. Look at the cast list of characters at the front of the play. Which could be described as 'round? Are there any which could be described as 'flat'?

2 From the list below, choose five words that you think best describe each character. Find a line from the text to support or evidence each of your choices.

Affectionate Ambitious Anxious Bitter Brave Calm Caring Childish Cold Competitive Content Conventional Cowardly Cruel Deceitful Difficult Dishonest Easy-going Energetic Free Generous Imaginative Immature Intelligent Irresponsible Irritable Jealous Kind Lonely Loving Loyal Misguided Obstinate Open-minded Paternal Playful Political Prejudiced Protective Proud Relaxed Resentful Resilient Responsible Restricted Sensible Strong Stubborn Warm Weak Wise

3 Which character in the play do you sympathize with most? And which least? Use evidence from the text to justify your reactions towards them.

4 The play's characters are given their own personalities and Sherriff wants his audience to be aware of the differences between them. However there are several moments where the role of the characters is more

functional and they speak in order to convey information about what has happened, or is happening off stage. This relaying of information to the audience is an important function of stage characters. Find some examples from the text where this happens.

5   Choose one character. Go through the play noting all the *stage directions* they are given. What conclusions can you draw about how the character's body is scripted over the whole play? What does it say about them?

Dramatic technique

Structure

One of the most common observations made about *Journey's End* when it premiered was that it was a ground-breaking play. J.T. Grein, an influential critic at the time, wrote in the *Illustrated London News* that Sherriff's 'methods are entirely away from hidebound rules. He proffers no plot, not even a continuous story. . . . All we see is life in the foul, cramped atmosphere of a dug-out' (15 December 1928, 11). It is true that the play *can* appear to be a series of loose episodes. In 1929, *The Times* likewise noted how 'the play is a series of scenes almost unrelated and as difficult of interpretation as they would be in real life' (22 January 1929, 10). As *The Times* noted, this was deliberate on Sherriff's part – he was trying to capture the haphazard nature of war. Just as in life, so in the play, things do not follow on from one another in a neat pattern. One event does not necessarily lead onto the next. Rather, Sherriff offers a series of snapshots of the relationships which have formed between the soldiers in the dugout.

However, what Sherriff *does* do is to introduce a number of *complications* or disruptions which interrupt the quiet moments and heighten the tension. One example is the arrival of Raleigh. His arrival then builds up to a mini climax ending with the discussion over the censored letter. This is resolved in Act Two and another complication is introduced – the sudden announcement of the raid. The next dramatic moment occurs with the confrontation between Stanhope and Hibbert. By the end of Act Two the audience is left waiting expectantly for the raid. In the first scene of Act Three, Osborne has died and there is a confrontation between Stanhope and Raleigh. Finally in the last scene there is the attack where Raleigh (and we assume the others) die.

Where the play is also unusual is that the audience is told what is going to happen. It is announced in the first moments that a big German attack is coming. Most of the audience of 1929 would have been able to remember something of the attack – it was part of their recent history – and would know what the fate of the soldiers was likely to be.

Language

Playwrights often have their own distinct style. This includes the language given to characters and the way in which conversations between characters are written. In the late nineteenth century Oscar Wilde's style included epigrams (short, witty sayings) which audiences came to expect. An example is 'I can resist everything except temptation' from *Lady Windermere's Fan* (1892). In the late twentieth century, Harold Pinter's plays became famous for the long pauses written into his characters' speeches.

It is difficult to spot any very striking features in R.C. Sherriff's work. There are no big chunks of speech as in one of Shakespeare's plays or witty sayings, as in Wilde's. What Sherriff *does* do is to uses short exchanges to suggest spontaneous speech.

Trotter How *are* you?
Raleigh Oh, all right, thanks.

Trotter Been out 'ere before?

Raleigh No.

Trotter Feel a bit odd, I s'pose?

Raleigh Yes. A bit.

Trotter (*getting a box to sit on*) Oh, well, you'll soon get used to it; you'll feel you've been 'ere a year in about an hour's time. (24)

One thing which is also worth noting is that this exchange is a reminder of the play's period and class origins. Most of the characters are officers who speak what is known as the Queen's English as it was understood in the 1920s. Norman Page has called Queen's English 'the conventional dialect of the heroic world' (*Speech in the English Novel*, 107). As the phrase suggests, this is the dialect spoken by the present Queen and which we also tend to see adopted as standard by gentlemanly heroes in British black and white films of the 1940s. Stanhope, Raleigh, Osborne, Hibbert and the Colonel share these same speech patterns. In contrast, the less-educated men like Trotter and Mason drop the letter 'h', indicating non-standard pronunciation. Mason is often played on stage as a cheerful Cockney. In Trotter's case his speech patterns also help denote his individuality – the other officers in the dugout do not speak like him.

Sherriff thus writes in a way which tries to suggest the accepted speech of the time and in particular the rhythms of conversation between men of a particular social class. 'The dialogue is authentic', wrote J.T. Grein in 1929, 'and to a soldier reminiscent to a degree which is almost painful' (*Tatler*, 30 January 1929, 214). Authenticity is difficult to prove, of course, but another way Sherriff tries to convince the audience is by scattering military references and slang through the text: support line, front line, gun position, Boche, No–Man's Land, Wipers, tochemmas, Phosgene, Vimy Ridge. This is Hardy describing an attack: 'Sometimes nothing happens for hours on end; then – all – of a sudden – over she comes! – rifle, grenades – Minnies' (10). The German trench-mortars were called mine-throwers (*Minenwerfer*) but were dubbed 'minnies' or 'Moaning minnies' (because of their sound) by the British. While it does not add to the plot to know that letters are collected by the quartermaster (as Osborne tells Raleigh (42)) it clearly does add to the audience's understanding of how day-to-day life on the front line worked. The audience learns, too, that men did not generally change their clothes or wash at the Front, as Osborne explains in Act One:

> **Osborne** We never undress when we're in the line. You can take your boots off now and then in the daytime, but it's better to keep pretty well dressed always.
> **Raleigh** I see. Thanks.
> **Osborne** I expect we shall each do about three hours on duty at a time and then six off. We all go on duty at stand-to. That's at dawn and dusk (20).

Similarly, hearing that the rifles need inspecting and oiling ('just the barrels and machines and all the metal parts' (47)) makes the atmosphere seem more genuine. Critics sometimes describe this kind of detail as 'the reality effect'. The phrase, which was first used by the French critic Roland Barthes in his essay 'The Reality Effect' (1968), refers to apparently small details – names, brands, topical references – which do not drive the action forward but give the text atmosphere, making it feel 'real'.

Also worth noting is that much of the dialogue in *Journey's End* can be labelled *colloquial*, i.e. it is informal. However, it is colloquialism of a particular time and place, i.e. most of it belongs to a middle-class speaker of the early twentieth century. In the 1920s a large part of the theatre audience was middle-class and in Sherriff's play they saw people like themselves or their friends on stage, something that presumably gave the play more impact. In his characters' dialogue Sherriff manages to given an impression of a familiar (to his audience) mixture of male speech – slangy, confident, educated. These are some examples:

Raleigh describing Stanhope: He was skipper of rugger at Barford, and kept wicket for the eleven. A jolly good bat, too. (17)

Hibbert: I don't think I can manage any supper tonight, Stanhope. It's this beastly neuralgia. (28)

Stanhope on Raleigh: He's a little prig. Wants to write home and tell Madge all about *me*. Well he won't d'you see Uncle? He *won't* write . . . (33).

When Stanhope confronts Hibbert: God! – you little swine. You know what that means – don't you? Striking a superior Officer! (56)

We can assume that not all young men spoke like this but what Sherriff creates is a carefully constructed casualness. It is not the same language that you would expect to see in a newspaper; it is *not* how people actually speak if we listen to them. Yet it is not too far from actual 1920s speech that an audience's sense that they are getting a glimpse of something life-like (or like life) will be disturbed. It seems un-self-conscious and Sherriff himself later explained that he tried to reproduce how people around him had spoken.

Having said all this, the language used by the characters can also seem a bit quaint or even laughable. It is as if we are stuck in a time capsule. The language can seem *too* polite, *too* chaste and *too* genteel. It is hard not think we are being offered a sanitized version of army life. There is hardly any bad language and certain topics which we assume soldiers (even officers) would talk about are rarely or never mentioned – class resentment and confrontation, women, prostitutes, sexually-transmitted disease, hygiene, injuries.

There is one obvious reason for this absence. Until 1968, the content of plays in Britain was still subject to censorship by the Lord Chamberlain. This was the senior representative in the Royal Household who, under the Stage Licensing Act, had the duty of approving new scripts before they could be licensed for public staging. A play with swearing or lots of sexual references would not be passed as suitable for performance. From what we know of R.C. Sherriff's own personality it is also highly unlikely that he would have dreamt of offending his audience and perhaps he conceived his gentlemanly characters as being too well-bred to swear anyhow. Nonetheless, despite the brief discussion of Hibbert's pornographic postcards and what seems to be an oblique reference to masturbation (82), it is probably safe to assume that we are given a sanitized version of trench life. What Sherriff gives the audience is a version of what Norman Page describes as *token speech*. This takes the form of 'conventionally and generally accepted substitutes for items of dialogue which would, in their 'straight' form, be regarded as unacceptable at a given time' (113).

Although *Journey's End* is notable for its plain language it is worth noting that sometimes Sherriff does have characters use language in an aesthetic way, that is to say, they use language which appeals to the senses. Thus Stanhope describes the landscape of 'No Man's Land' as being 'all churned up like a sea that's got muddier and muddier till it's so stiff that it can't move' (45). The words help convey a sense of off-stage space and the conditions in which the soldiers have to fight. Sometimes men drowned in the mud. However Stanhope's words also have a *figurative* usage and describe the personal situations of the play's characters. They, too, are 'churned up', trapped, swamped by the war and about to be sent under.

Sherriff also makes use of metaphor. A metaphor is a word or phrase being used to designate another apparently unrelated thing. A famous example is 'All the world's a stage/And all the men and women merely players' from Shakespeare's *As You Like It*. Shakespeare makes a comparison but also wants his audience to see human experience in a new light. In *Journey's End*, an apparently innocent exchange at the beginning of Act One provides a powerful example of Sherriff's use of metaphor. Hardy explains the rules of earwig racing, an apparently popular hobby amongst his men: 'Oh, you each have an earwig, and start 'em in a line. On the word "Go" you dig your earwig in the ribs and steer him with a match across the table. I won ten francs last night – had a *splendid* earwig'(15).

Hardy then lets Osborne into a secret. '[I]f you want to get the best pace out of an earwig, dip it in whiskey – makes 'em go like hell!' (15). As well as giving the audience information about things soldiers did to pass the time, Sherriff has also made Hardy describe the fate of the soldiers – they are also earwigs waiting to be made to go, starting 'in a line' before they clamber out of the trenches on the attack. There is also a reference to Stanhope; he, too, needs a 'dip' in whisky before he can do anything.

Things to do

1 Select a moment from the text which depicts class difference. Suggest how Sherriff gives his characters different vocabularies and ways of speaking to emphasize the differences between the men.

2 Pick out five words or phrases in which Sherriff makes use of specialist military vocabulary or slang. Research these, making sure you know what they mean.

3 Select a conversation from the text where the main purpose seems to be to give the audience an insight into the workings of trench life.

Design

Any reading of *Journey's End* needs to include consideration of the stage and the space in which the play takes place. One term for the way in which a play is staged is *mis-en-scène*, a French phrase that means 'placing on stage' and includes the actors, lighting, décor, props, costumes. All ingredients work together to convey meaning, establish character and develop themes.

You will see that in the case of *Journey's End*, the play's opening stage directions provide a detailed description of the play's setting. Obviously, the way in which the play's setting is represented depends on the theatre in which it is being performed but from Sherriff's stage directions it seems apparent that he had in mind a *box-set* familiar in twentieth century theatre and often used to depict interiors (three sides of a room and open to the audience on the fourth). The stage is scripted to appear closed-in and claustrophobic:

> A *few rough steps lead to the trench above, through a low doorway. A table occupies a good space of the dugout floor. A wooden frame, covered with wire netting, stands against the left wall and serves the double purpose of a bed and a seat for the table. A wooden bench against the back wall makes another seat, and two boxes serve the other sides.*
>
> *Another wire-covered bed is fixed in the right corner beyond the doorway.*
>
> *Gloomy tunnels lead out of the dugout to left and right.*
>
> *Except for the tables, beds and seats, there is no furniture save the bottles holding the candles, and a few tattered magazine pictures pinned to the wall of girls in flimsy costumes . . .*
>
> *Through the doorway can be seen the misty grey parapet of a trench and a narrow strip of starlit sky. A bottle of whisky, a jar of water, and a mug stand on the table amongst a litter of papers and magazines.* (8–9)

This is the only setting in *Journey's End*. As an environment it is cramped. It lacks privacy and cleanliness and despite their repeated entrances and exits, the characters are trapped in it. It is possible that Sherriff wants the audience to experience it not only visually but by *kinaesthetic* means, that is to say, understand it via physical sensation and bodily reaction. In the original production people were struck by the noise of gun fire and shelling created on stage. Some modern productions deliberately stage the play in small theatres to intensify the effect of claustrophobic conditions.

From this opening scene the audience is made aware that the dugout is below ground because the soldiers enter down the stairs. This underground setting is symbolic of hell or imprisonment and perhaps even foreshadows the men's deaths – they have dug, and are living in, a mass grave. We might also argue that because the men are below ground, they are out of sight but also out of mind. They risk being forgotten about, both by those in command and by the British public. Sherriff's aim in writing his play is to excavate them and bring them back into the light.

Whilst the set on stage remains the same, it is important to remember that there is an *offstage* space. This is made up of the trenches, and beyond that, 'No Man's Land', and beyond that, the German lines. The other direction leads to the British bases. The stairs connect the dugout with the trench. This offstage space has a direct relationship with the onstage space and at various moments in the play the audience is asked to think about the offstage space and what is happening there. Sometimes we are told about it, as in the case of the raid and Osborne's death. However, shelling and gun fire are also the sounds of war and they periodically interrupt what is happening in the onstage space. Act One ends with '*the low rumble of distant guns*' being heard '*[t]hrough the stillness*' as the men try to sleep (35).

When the play premiered some observers suggested that Sherriff was helped by the fact that in 1928 most people had an idea of what the trenches were like. They would have read other material about the war and seen films and could picture the other unseen soldiers. The result, as Ivor Brown noted, was that Sherriff did 'not have to create . . . on a blank table of the mind the terrible event or tragic environment' (*Saturday Review*, 16 January 1929, 107). The audience could imagine what lay at the top of the dug-out stairs. For some it was a sight they had experienced first-hand.

Lighting

Depending upon the design required by the play, lighting is tool for establishing mood as well as time of day. In the opening scene, Sherriff directs that there should be a '*pale glimmer of moonlight [which] shines down the narrow steps into one corner of the dugout*' and refers to the '*[w]arm yellow candle-flames*' which '*light the other corner from the necks of two bottles on the table*' (9). Despite the battlefront location, the mood is not immediately threatening.

The dugout, of course, is never light. Act Two begins with the direction '*A pale shaft of sunlight shines down the steps but candles still burn in the dark corner where Osborne and Raleigh are at breakfast*' (36). It is morning but artificial light is still needed. It is also possible that the still-burning candles are intended to remind the audience that the events of the previous evening are still fresh and unresolved – they have not been extinguished. Later, Raleigh's death occurs as '*[a] very faint rose light is beginning to glow in the dawn sky*' (93) and there is a stark contrast between the beauty of the dawn and the ugliness of the slaughter.

It is worth noting, too, that at the end of a scene a dimming of lights conveys both the passing of time and notifies the audience that it is the end of the scene. At other moments soft lighting (candles) is used to suggest the dugout as a place of refuge – even cosiness. In some productions directors have also used lighting to suggest states of mind. For example, they have Stanhope move into the shadows on stage when he wants to conceal himself suggesting that there are parts of himself he will never reveal.

Sound

Like lighting, sound is a way of establishing the setting, and in the case of *Journey's End*, fighting happening offstage. The most striking example of this is in Act Three, Scene One where the audience does not see but hears the raid. Sherriff provides very detailed stage directions. The initial silence is followed by *'the dull "crush" of bursting smoke bombs'*, the *'whistle'*, *'whine'* and *'crash'* of shells and the *'rattle'* of machine guns (73).

Costumes

Visual indications of the play's period are also shown in the characters' costumes. Not surprisingly the soldiers wear British army uniforms of the First World War. For the initial production in 1928 some of the cast had served in the army and dug out their own uniforms to wear. Sherriff lent Laurence Olivier (who played Stanhope) his tunic together with his revolver and holster. The uniforms worn by the characters designate their rank. We might expect Raleigh's uniform to be pristine compared to those worn by the long-serving soldiers. The National Army Museum has images of the kind of clothing soldiers wore on its website.[13] Surrey Heritage, which holds the archives of R.C. Sherriff, has also posted online photos of the actors in costume in the 1929 production.[14]

Props and objects

The props and objects used within the play are important in understanding Sherriff's thinking. For example, we see Stanhope's bottle of whisky when the lights come up on the first scene. Other props are also permanent fixtures. The table is a place for regular meals where the characters come together as a substitute family. Also significant are the magazine pin-ups on the wall which remind us of the absence of real female

---

[13] http://www.army.mod.uk/firstworldwarresources/

[14] http://www.exploringsurreyspast.org.uk/themes/subjects/military/surreys-first-world-war/

company. This is an all-male environment and women are present only to be leered at or written to (as in the case of Raleigh's sister and Osborne's wife).

Another prop that acquires a powerful emotional significance is Raleigh's letter to his sister in Act Two, Scene One. Raleigh plans to leave the letter for collection but is ordered by Stanhope to 'leave it open' (47). Stanhope's unease about Raleigh's arrival is represented by his attitude towards the letter. As he panics over the contents, the stage directions instruct him to grab Raleigh by the wrist and rip the letter out of his hand, only to discover that his fears have been unfounded.

A second key moment which highlights the emotional weight of objects within the play is the sequence in Act Three, Scene One where, prior to the raid, Osborne and Raleigh empty their pockets of papers. The reason for this is so that, if captured, the enemy will not get any extra information about the men or their plans. However, Osborne also takes off his wedding ring and watch to pass onto his wife if he should die, together with a farewell letter. Like Raleigh's letter, all these objects represent ties to family and to the past but they also embody emotions and feelings which cannot be spoken out loud, certainly not in the dugout. The wedding ring is a symbol of Osborne's love for his wife, as well as a reminder to the audience that Mrs Osborne, as a widow, will be another casualty of war.

Critical reception

One of the issues worth considering is *Journey's End*'s reception history and its meaning for different generations of readers and playgoers. It is clearly significant that one section of current critical opinion presents Sherriff's play as very much 'of its time', i.e. the 1920s, whilst another section finds in it the potential to speak to the anxieties and interests of the later twentieth and then twenty-first centuries.

When *Journey's End* opened at London's Savoy Theatre in January 1929 several reviewers hailed the play as a masterpiece. This was mostly on account of what Alan Parsons, writing in the *Daily Mail*, termed its 'absolute *reality*'. '[I]t is all there – the suffering, the blank misery, the comradeship, the unconquerable humour, the nobility and heroism' (22 January, 10). Parsons' comments were echoed by others who had served in the war (W.A. Darlington's comments were quoted earlier (p.27)).

The play also seemed to show the war in a way which was new and above all, honest. The *Daily News and Westminster Gazette* suggested that *Journey's End* would 'make us understand their minds' and 'the common lot of our soldiers' (22 January 1929, 5). In turn, people who *had* fought felt that Sherriff was helping by giving them a voice which, as they saw it, had not been done on stage before. Thus one of the reasons why the play received a positive response is that it tried to treat the wartime experience responsibly and without silliness. Richard Jennings, writing in the *Spectator*, suggested that 'one may compare *Journey's End*, which conveys no deliberate message, and attempts no propaganda, to the similarly faithful and quiet record of Mr Edmund Blunden's *Undertones of War*[15]. This too, is written with the same unobtrusive art – tunnelling as it were, under the surface of sensational events' (2 February 1929, 154). This was also a point made by the *Daily Express* which suggested that the play 'shows life at the front, with an unemotional realism which is a much better argument against war than sentimental propaganda plays' (23 January 1929, 9). Other critics simply marvelled at how a play so apparently uncommercial, with no women or attractive costumes and sets, managed to get on stage in the first place.

One of the things that perplexed audiences – as it has done ever since – was the issue of the play's message. Some critics, as

---

[15] Edmund Blunden's memoir of the war published in 1928.

the comments above indicate, decided that the play did not have one. Ivor Brown, the *Saturday Review*'s reviewer, argued that R.C. Sherriff,

> is no lecturer; his war-play does not beat the drum-didactic. He is obviously concerned to be accurate and, though his subject concerns the ghastly monotony of life in the catacombs and cellarage of war as well as the flourishes and alarums above ground, he obviously succeeds in being exciting. But he is exciting not in the . . . crook-play sense of showing people filthily killed, but in the genuine dramatist's sense of showing them vividly alive.

For Brown this was where the play gained power. The audience gets to know the characters – they even become fond of them as they might do real people – and because of this feel the waste of their deaths. Brown also argued that despite the very particular setting and realistic details, Sherriff was dealing with timeless subject matter. The play was as powerful as the tales of ancient Troy and Viking legends and its men were as heroic as the warriors of old – and as helpless in the face of forces they cannot control. The difference was that Osborne and the others were not honoured in death:

> When the play closes Osborne is a shattered corpse outside and Raleigh is lying dead within; over his body the dugout begins to collapse under shell-fire. There are no funerals with military honours here . . . For Osborne and Raleigh there is only the swallowing and consuming earth over which the slaughterous scramble goes pauseless on . . . their funeral offerings are just more broken bodies of boys, more dust to more dust, waste without end. (26 January 1929, 106)

Not everyone was as impressed or moved. The 1920s also saw the rise of socialism in Britain and the emergence of the Labour Party as a potent political force. The *New Statesman*, a magazine long connected with the socialist Fabian society, occupied a position on the left of the political spectrum. Not surprisingly, its (class conscious) reviewer had a slightly different take on the play's outlook and its cast of – as he saw it – dim public schoolboys:

> The theme is the nerve strain of the firing line on various kinds of soldier, but all the fighting takes place off the stage. Though superbly acted, this seems definitely a play which cannot be appreciated unless you have fought in the war. It is an orgy of the public school spirit. . . . A very typical scene is where Hibbert, the shirker, who has been persuaded not to run away, Stanhope and the ranker [Trotter] celebrate together. All begin to boast about women but when the unfortunate Hibbert takes Stanhope at his word, and begins to recount a genuine amorous adventure, he is promptly sat on as a dirty-minded little beast, after the best traditions of the prefects' room. . . .
>
> The effect on the spectator who has not been through the war himself is to produce a seething impatience with the idiotic little colonel and his talk of putting up a good show, the hopeless loyalty of bovine sergeant majors . . . and so on, up to the invisible, and, though probably not modest, equally schoolboy brigadier. The essence of the war was its stupidity, the wasteful stupidity of the wholesale holocaust of valuable lives: surely a play could emphasise this by giving the victims articulation and intelligence. Was the war really only a slaughterhouse for athletes and a school for gentlemen?
>
> 'C.C.', 'Journeys End', New Statesman,
2 February 1929, 531

Recently, Jay Winter and Antoine Prost have argued that literature written in the 1920s helped create a distorted 'history of the war . . . without trench soldiers', that is, it was entirely focused on the officer class (*The Great War in History*, 83). This is not a new charge. As the *New Statesman*'s critic saw it in 1929, this version of the war is precisely what *Journey's End* helped encourage – and some would say, still does.

Things to do

While most critics thus found *Journey's End* to be extremely emotionally involving, and were much more prepared than the characters on stage to cry, the play was also controversial.

Below are two extracts taken from reviews by H.T.W. Bousefield in *The English Review* and R. Dawson in the same magazine. They show something of the debate the play prompted when it first appeared. Your task is to:

- Read the extract, using a dictionary to help you with any words that are unfamiliar.

- Summarize in a sentence or two the argument put forward in each extract.

- In two columns **Attack** and **Support**, jot down any words or phrases that are used to either attack or support Sherriff's play.

H.T.W. Bousefield, '*Journey's End*. Another Point of View', *The English Review* (October 1929), 491–6

Any play that pretends to be in some sort history is more than a casual entertainment; it has a definite effect upon the public who go to see it. After many months of unvarying success the public that has seen *Journey's End* has grown to considerable dimensions. Great numbers of ordinary men and women, young and old, have seen it and gone quietly away, and 'everybody who is anybody' has seen it too, and gone away to proclaim its wonders, its truth, its force, its – every approving epithet that is fashionable at the moment. The play is a sensation, just as a bull fight is a sensation . . . .

I have no fault to find with the technique of *Journey's End*. It is a very clever play indeed. The dozens of managers who, one is informed, rejected it, have only themselves to thank for losing a fortune. In fact it is hard to understand how anybody ... could have failed to recognize its money-making qualities – and equally hard to believe that the abysmally bad taste of the thing could have been responsible for its rejection.

Journey's End is the worst exhibition of bad taste that this century has seen, and it is tasteless in the way that murder is tasteless and matricide ill-bred.

Does anyone believe that such a sustained insult to our armies would have been tolerated by the nation even five years ago? In 1919, what theatre presenting *Journey's End* could have escaped the just fury of its audience? In those days the show would have been pelted, smashed, abolished. It survives today because we have mislaid our self-respect; because it provides a kick for sensationalists who have lost their palate . . . .

Twelve countries, one is informed, are staging *Journey's End*. Have twelve nations lost their wits? Or are twelve nations enjoying the spectacle of a demoralized Britain? Twelve countries, anyway; but one that has lately established manhood as a popular ideal, rejects it. Mussolini's Italy has banned *Journey's End*. Mussolini is the only authority who has discerned its implications: That there is no such thing as heroism. That brave deeds are performed by accident, by force of circumstances stronger than the hero, by a spirit of alcoholic despair refreshed at intervals by lewdness.

No one in these days desires to see war glorified; it has no glory. No one desires to hear that the sacrifice of manhood to war is necessary or, from any point of view, desirable. . . . But *Journey's End* is not only untrue . . . [i]ts success as a maker of profits at the expense of memories, that hitherto our nation has held sacred, is a circumstance of shame that would astound a pessimist.

How many fathers, mothers, wives and even sweethearts still cherish their love for someone who went out to that hell of war and did not return? Surely a great multitude. How many believed – until the appearance of *Journey's End* – in the sheer courage and nobility of spirit of the man or boy who had made the sunshine warm for them? And how many who have seen it can keep their ideal?

There are two outstanding characters in the play. One is a coward whose fear has dominated his whole existence, the other a hero whose heroism is mere drunken despair. . . . *Journey's End* is, however, supposed to be a starkly true and realistic picture of our own men who won the greatest war of all time. If it were true and realistic, what sort of creatures must our enemies have been?

We complain of the iconoclastic tendencies of this post-war generation. We fill our newspapers with irritable articles about the lack of ideals and reverence in the young, their looseness of conduct, their sexual opportunism. And then, to show them the truth about heroism, we present *Journey's End*! We show them what appears to be a proof that every moral splendour is a sham. If these young people laugh when they see the play, upon my soul it is not the comic batman who amuses them but their pompous elders who have let themselves be found out!

. . . . There was a time when national honour and personal honour were hotly defended, and man who did not hold his honour sacred, and his country's honour as his own, was thought unworthy of citizenship in any human society. Surely the honour of the million dead who died in the war for the rest of us, is still a thing beyond profits. What a pitch of emasculation have we reached that it should be possible for *Journey's End* to be not only tolerated but acclaimed?

If we are not to become a race of gigolos, it is time to produce an antidote to this necrosis of the soul.

R. Dawson, '*Journey's End*. A Supplementary Estimate', *The English Review*, (November 1929), 620–3

Dawson begins by linking Sherriff's play with another controversial best-seller, German author, Erich Remarque's novel, *All Quiet on the Western Front* (1929). This is another grim depiction of life in the trenches told from the point of view of a young soldier (see p.82).

Herr E.M. Remarque's *All Quiet on the Western Front* and Mr. R.C. Sherriff's *Journey's End* have received wider and more spontaneous appreciation, coupled with narrower and more shallow criticism, than has been accorded to any work for many years. Each man in his own way has shown us the reality of modern warfare, and has exposed it as an animal reality, brutish, bestial and degraded. . . . They have pared it clean of romance and of the accretions of sentimentality. They have shown us war stark war, stark war. The two works have been translated into every important European language, impression after impression has been sold, performance after performance has been applauded. Are we to throw puny criticism in the face of this? Are we to call the reading and play-going public of Europe deluded and degenerate? Are we to condemn every rank of society of base ingratitude and sensation-mongering? Is it now criminal to face facts? Let us strip off all the sentimentality which we assumed during the war, and without which those four years would have been unendurable. Let us dissipate the mists of romance existing in the minds of those who are beginning to forget, and of those who never knew. And what have we? Heroes? One or two. Men? Millions. . . .

There is no more point in calling the men who went to fight heroes than there is in saying they had two legs. . . . Heroism used to imply sacrifice transcending the immediate exactions of duty; during the war it was applied to every man who answered duty's call. But how many of those men felt in their hearts that they were heroes? That idea was left for sentimentality-mongers. . . . In a sense, of course, every man who fought was a hero – someone's hero, some village's hero . . . but when we see the thing as a whole, where is the heroism? It is where Mr Sherriff has perceived it, in the heart of a man whose sensibilities threaten to overwhelm his physical courage, and yet whose spiritual integrity and inbred sense of duty demand inexorably the stopping up of every access of weakness. Stanhope stands firm as the supreme example of the heroism which many men were called upon to express. He knew that his finer feelings and sensitive nerves had no place in an environment of bestial slaughter. . . . Yet he knew that his country's safety rested on the successful issue of war, and so he made the greatest sacrifice a man can make; the sacrifice of his higher self. Then only was he able to fulfil his obligations to his country. If this is not heroism, then God knows what is! But it was the heroism of civilized man, not of the man who neither thought nor felt, but of a man who realized and suffered. . . . In Hibbert we have a man who was incapable of the understanding by which he might have adjusted himself to circumstances, and circumstances nearly overcame him. Yet when the crisis came, he stood to it like a man. And what of the rest? – Osborne, Trotter, Raleigh, the amusing batman, and the rest of the whole company of men who filed along the trench to their appointed places to meet a bloody dawn?

Let not . . . ignorant criticism prejudice the understanding of this play, for it is great work, artistically and spiritually. Instead, let every man and woman look into the soul of Stanhope with sympathy and discernment, and when they have seen a civilized man shattered by war, when they have seen the ghastly fatuity of it all, the degradation and futility, we shall have an argument stronger than patriotism, and more universal than the League of Nations. We shall have an argument based on a common understanding of civilized humanity.

Commentary

There are many aspects you may have picked out of these extracts, but here are some things to note:

1   The two critics differ greatly in their response to the play. Bousefield thinks *Journey's End* an insult to those men who fought in the war. It is in 'bad taste'. Dawson, on the other hand, sees the play as providing an

important corrective to the tendency to mythologize the war and those who took part. He writes of the 'mists of romance' which the play helps sweep away.

2　Bousefield hates Sherriff's depiction of Hibbert and Stanhope because it suggests that the soldiers were either cowards or drunkards. He suggests that this not only a disloyal representation of the dead but is an unhelpful message to send to the current generation of young people – particularly young men – of post-war Britain. It will undermine their respect for the men who died. Dawson meanwhile suggests that men who were frightened, like Hibbert, were still heroes for conquering their fears and going through to the end. He singles out Stanhope as the 'supreme example' the kind of heroism demanded of soldiers.

3　Bousefield thinks that the play is exploiting the dead for commercial gain. There is something wrong with the playwright for writing this sort of work and with those people who ghoulishly who go to see it. He compares it to a bull fight or sightseeers gathering round the scene of a murder. Dawson, on the other hand, sees *Journey's End* as a play carrying out important humanitarian work, encouraging recognition for those who died but also helping the cause of peace. He even suggests that it is much more effective than the League of Nations. This was the international organization, headquartered in Geneva, Switzerland, created in 1920 as a body for sorting out international disputes and to ensure that the unprecedented slaughter of the 1914–1918 war never happened again.

The final extracts in this section come from four recent critics. As you read, decide whether you agree with them or not. Can you find evidence in the play to support or challenge what they say?

John Onions, *English Fiction and Drama of the Great War, 1918–39* (Basingstoke: Macmillan, 1990), 92

Journey's End was one of the greatest commercial successes of interwar British theatre ... It received extravagant praise at the time. ... However the high claims for it have not endured; it is clear, that, far from being a realistic attack on the [concept of the] hero; it asserts heroic duty.

Steven Trout, 'Glamorous Melancholy': R.C. Sherriff's *Journey's End*, *War, Literature and the Arts* 2:1 (Fall/Winter 1993), 3–18

Sherriff's drama, and its reception, suggest something of the equivocal and contradictory nature of war experience itself. Although Sherriff ostensibly exposed the horrors of the Western Front through his suffering hero, Dennis Stanhope, the play evaded the anti-heroic conclusions implicit in Stanhope's tragic story and betrayed a nostalgic longing for life in the 'old Front line', a longing apparently shared by Sherriff's audience. The play reminds us that horror and revulsion ... were only two of the complex and often contradictory reactions of British veterans to their service in the Great War (3).

Heinz Kosok, *The Theatre of War. The First World War in British and Irish Drama* (Basingstoke, 2007), 158

There is little in the text to provoke an anti-war attitude, unless the reader or spectator comes to the play predisposed to see it in such a light ... [T]he War as such is never brought into perspective.

John Gross, 'Dead Eyes Behind', *Sunday Telegraph*, 25 January 2004

The play packs in a great deal about the circumstances of the war and the spirit of the men caught up in it. But when it touches on such large topics as comradeship, or courage, or the shortcomings of the top brass, it mostly does so through small confrontations and casual remarks.... The men are individuals, not representative types – though by the end we do feel that they have acquired a symbolic value, and that this small corner of the war can also stand for the war as a whole. The play also commemorates the gentlemanly ethos of a bygone England, in all its strengths and limitations.

Related works

It is useful to compare *Journeys End* with other writings about the war published at about the same time. The play was part of what we might call a 'cultural conversation' about the First World War and its effects. Although it began in the 1920s, it is a conversation still happening today.

All Quiet on the Western Front (Erich Maria Remarque, 1929)

Erich Maria Remarque's novel *All Quiet on the Western Front* was published as a book in Germany in January 1929 and became a world-wide hit. Like R.C. Sherriff, Remarque had served as a soldier – albeit in the German army – and the novel has been seen to be based on some of his war-time experiences. It has a teenager, Paul, as its narrator who, with his friends, has been persuaded into enlisting by his school teacher with the promise of great adventure. What they encounter is nothing like what they expected and the novel is full of the gruesome detail, as well the absurdities, of life at the Front. The novel is more obviously angry than *Journey's End* in its accusations of the betrayal of the younger generation. It also avoids the officer-favouritism of Sherriff's play. But Remarque does recreate many of the same things: the comradeship of the lost generation, the young officer admired by the soldiers; the men's powerlessness, the details of trench life; the cynicism and black humour used to cope with horrible situations; a feeling that those at home have no real idea about what goes on and continue to believe in vague ideas about heroism and honour.

All Quiet on the Western Front does not offer a complete or comprehensive record but it is a valuable point of comparison with *Journey's End*. Like Sherriff's play it was read as an anti-war or pacifist piece of work. Remarque denied the pacifist intent, although this did not stop the novel being banned by the Nazis in the 1930s.

The Silver Tassie (Sean O'Casey, 1929)

The Silver Tassie by Sean O'Casey (1880–1964) opened at the Apollo Theatre in London on 11 October 1929. O'Casey said that the play was written partially as a response to *Journey's End* which, as he saw it, offered a sickly, sentimental approach to war. O'Casey was accused of being jealous of Sherriff's success but for him *Journey's End* glamourized the war. He condemned its 'false affrontery ... which made of war a pleasant thing to see and feel'. Sherriff had ignored the horrors of the war turning it into

a demure echo, told under candlelight, at a gentle fireside ... a discreet accompaniment to a strident song, done on a lute, played low; the stench of blood hid in a mist of soft-sprayed perfume; the yells of agony modulated down to a sweet pianissimo of pain; surly death exultant, fashioned into a smiling courtier, bringing himself in with a bow; a balmy breath of blood and guts; all the mighty, bloodied vulgarity or war foreshortened into a pretty, pleasing picture.

SEAN O'CASEY, *Autobiographies* II
(London: 1963) 335

Because it overlapped with *Journey's End*, *The Silver Tassie* was immediately compared to it (usually unfavourably). Typically for him, O'Casey's play is about Irish subjects. It is set at the height of the war which O'Casey saw as a war of aggression, rather than as one of defence. The play follows two young footballers from the slums of Dublin through the battlefields of France, and their subsequent return. The Silver Tassie of the title is a silver cup which becomes symbolic of the simple life Harry Heegan lives before the war breaks out. In the first act, set in the family home, his parents wait for him to return from a Gaelic football match. He arrives triumphant, carried on the shoulders of his team mates, holding the trophy. When the play ends Harry is a victim of the war, paralyzed from the waist down. The play is thus partly about loss and in one of its climatic moments, Harry smashes the trophy to the ground – a reminder of the man he no longer is.

For Services Rendered (W. Somerset Maugham, 1932)

This play is set fifteen years after the end of the First World War in the home of the middle-class Ardsley family living in Kent. The play's comfortable, domestic setting is deceptive because what looks to be a gentle comedy turns into a kind of mental bloodbath as a succession of characters reveal how badly they have been damaged by the war. The audience is drawn into the misery of unhappy marriages, mental breakdowns, infidelity, sex, suicide, death and despair, all of which are at odds with the dream of a post-war 'land fit for heroes'. Particularly notable is the eldest daughter, Eva, still mourning her fiancée (killed in the war) and frustrated at how her life has turned out. As an unmarried daughter she is expected to look after her brother Sydney (blinded in the war). At the end of the play Eva's frustration drives her to madness. The play's title, like that of *Journey's End*, provides a bitter comment on the theme of the play.

In 1932, *For Services Rendered* was attacked for its pessimism. In response Maugham explained that he wrote the play because he was worried about 'this muddle of a post-war world', in particular the rise of the Nazis: 'every moment we see the countries of Europe arming themselves to the teeth as hard as they can go and that is why I wrote my play . . . to try and protect the new youth of today from dying in the trenches or losing five years of their lives in a war that seems almost imminent' (*Daily Express*, 3 November 1932).

Glossary of dramatic terms[16]

Act   The subdivision between sections of a play. Acts are subdivided further into Scenes.

Actor   A person (male or female) who is to play a character other than his/her own.

Blocking   The process of arranging moves to be made by the actors during the play, based on the stage directions.

Character   Generally, a named individual within the world of the play. Can also refer to the mental and moral qualities of an individual.

Characterization   The art of creating character. Within the play text characters can be presented via description from other characters, via stage directions or via descriptions written by the playwright, all of which the actor must try to convey physically or via their speech.

Conflict   A device set up by the playwright. There are four main types of conflict

   (a) Relational. This a battle or disagreement between one
        character and another character.

---

[16] Source: Theatre Crafts. Entertainment Technology Resources. http://www. theatrecrafts.com/glossaryofterms

(b) Societal. Occurs between the individual (or a group) and a larger group or society itself.

(c) Inner conflict. A character struggles with him or herself, and tries to escape a way of behaving (addition) or frame of mind.

(d) Situational conflict. Involving a situation which must be escaped or resolved.

Costumes   The clothes worn by the actors on stage.

Dialogue   The spoken text of a play – conversations between characters is called dialogue.

Director   The person responsible for the overall vision of a production. S/he will make practical decisions about how the play is to be done. In his autobiography R.C. Sherriff makes it clear that the play's first director, James Whale (who also designed the play's set), was key to its success.

Exposition   The section of plot at the start of the play which provides essential information about the characters, their situation and their relationship to each other.

Playwright   The author of a play, also known as a dramatist.

Plot   The basic story thread running through a play which gives the reasons for the characters' actions.

Props   Furnishings, large and small items which cannot be classified as scenery or costume. Props handled by the actors are known as hand props, for example Raleigh's letter.

Proxemics   Meaning the distances between characters on stage. It shows their relationships and feelings. For example if two characters stood far apart from each other the audience could assume they did not know each other or had fallen out.

Realism   In the theatre this describes a decision by the creative team to give the audience an accurate depiction of the real world rather than a stylized interpretation.

Realization   The physical manifestation of a play on stage.

Script   The text of a play or musical; also contains stage directions.

Set   The complete stage setting for a scene or act.

Setting   The place where the world of the play happens. The set represents the setting.

Stage directions   Instructions given by the author about how a play should be staged, how actors should move, enter and exit, and how lines should be said. For example: '**Stanhope** [*laughing and helping himself to a drink*]: You going to have one?' (46).

Subtext   The content of a play or novel or film which is not announced explicitly but is something the audience becomes aware of as the story progresses. One sub-text of *Journey's End* could be said to be the incompetence of those in charge of running the war.

CHAPTER TWO

Behind the Scenes

Do we need to know anything about the events behind a play? How it came into being? Who wrote it? There are different views on this. Some people would argue 'yes': we do need to know something about the playwright or playmaker behind the play, it can give extra insight into events or characters. Others would argue that while details about William Shakespeare's, Oscar Wilde's, or R.C. Sherriff's lives might be noteworthy, they are not really important in reading the play in question and can be distracting. This is a decision you have to make yourself as a critic. This section is designed to give you some ideas by focusing on the play's author, R.C. Sherriff and its first director, James Whale.

R. C. Sherriff (playwright)

In the 1920s one question which people often asked was: whether it was actually possible to write about the First World War? Could words ever express its horrors? The need to put some distance between themselves and the events of the war is one reason why it took many writers ten years before they felt able to write about it

Another issue was: *who* should do the writing? There was one section of people who thought that only those who had fought in the war themselves were qualified to write about it.

There was an 'us versus them' mentality, with 'us' being those who had seen action – and thus knew what they were talking about – and 'them' being the ones who had stayed at home. This mind set persisted for a long time. There was a feeling that women – even if they were amongst those nursing with the Voluntary Aid Detachments at the Front – would always be excluded from part of the action. Vera Brittain, whose *Testament of Youth* is one of the great autobiographical accounts of the war, recalled this sense that there was something obscene about women presuming to understand the conflict. This feeling, she recalled, was 'rooted in the contention that men die for their country but women do not ('War Service in Perspective', 375). Just as the trench was a forbidden zone to women, so, too, the war was considered as exclusively male and involving male relationships – an experience from which women were excluded. As is often noted, there are no women on stage in *Journey's End* apart from those on the walls and on the postcards in Hibbert's pocket.

This way of thinking offers one route into understanding *Journey's End*, that is, via its author Robert Cedric Sherriff (1896–1975). Sherriff had been part of this male world and his credentials for writing a war play were in these respects excellent. At the time Britain declared war on Germany, Sherriff was an insurance clerk living with his parents at Hampton Wick, a village south-west of London on the banks of the River Thames. He was an enthusiastic member of Kingston Rowing Club. In November 1915 he enlisted and managed to get an army commission, that is to say, he joined as a trainee officer, not as an 'ordinary' soldier. As we have seen, one of the criticisms made of *Journey's End* is that the play is almost entirely about the experience of officers, rather than the soldiers they commanded and it could be argued that Sherriff is offering us a very one-sided view of the war-time experience.

After training Sherriff saw active service in France as a lieutenant in the 9th East Surrey Regiment from September 1916 to August 1917. Some accounts suggest that Sherriff hated his experiences as a soldier and that he tried to get himself discharged rather like Hibbert does in the play. Eventually Sherriff was injured in the face and hand at the battle of Passchendaele (1917) when a shell exploded. After hospitalization he remained in the army helping train recruits. By the time he was released in January 1919 he had achieved the rank of Captain. He then went back to work for his previous employer, the insurance company.

The outline of Sherriff's life and writing career after the war remains slightly shadowy but in some ways very familiar. In career terms there was a sense of immense promise embodied in the writing of *Journey's End*, a strong sense of commitment, a willingness to take risks, a flurry of productivity for roughly twenty years (1930–1950) and then gradual silence. Children did not take over; there is no record of Sherriff having had any romantic relationships with women or men. He bought a Rolls Royce and a house in Esher, Surrey and lived there with his mother until she died and after that, on his own. Sherriff's wealth was proof of the enormous success of *Journey's End*. What Sherriff – despite all the interviews he gave – actually thought about anything apart from rowing remains a mystery. Was he lonely? He was very famous in the 1930s and 1940s but by the time he died in 1975 he had been forgotten by many people.

It was different in the beginning. In 1931, following the success of *Journey's End*, the young R.C. Sherriff wrote a best-selling novel, *The Fortnight in September*, about an ordinary suburban family whose uneventful lives proved incredibly popular with readers. When Sherriff began to write more plays, he approached the task in a similar vein, trying to produce works which celebrated 'Englishness' and traditional values. A play about the polar explorer Captain Robert Scott did not get finished but *Badger's Green* (1930) did and became the eagerly awaited sequel to *Journey's End*. The play is a comedy about a group of village people obsessed with cricket. Another successful play was *Windfall* (1934), about a male shop assistant who wins the lottery but is made miserable by his good fortune and grasping family: 'a faithful character study of middle-class life, if at times depressing', was *The New York Times*'s verdict on this story about 'simple people'. The same newspaper noted, too, that it had 'none of the gripping intensity of his [Sherriff's] war success' (27 February 1934). This was a regular complaint: nothing Sherriff did afterwards could match up to *Journey's End*.

Sherriff returned to the traumas of war in *St Helena* (1936), a historical play focusing on the exile and death of the Emperor Napoleon, but when it premiered the play was not very popular. More successful was *Home at Seven* (1950) which saw Sherriff back on safer ground, his 'modest intentions . . . completely fulfilled' claimed *The Times*, in this play about a bank clerk who loses his memory and thinks he may have committed a murder (8 March 1950, 2). Throughout his career Sherriff was praised for his ability to capture 'the humdrum and repetitive idiom' of his characters' lives – just as he was for *Journey's End*. Yet Sherriff's fondness for small details – his characters spend a lot of time eating meals and drinking tea – did not please everybody and there was criticism of his persistent refusal to tackle bigger issues. In terms of twentieth-century theatre history, Sherriff remains a figure on the margins; with the exception of *Journey's End*, his work is generally seen to be of limited importance. As *The Times's* comments (cited above) imply he was seen as someone who was small-scale. There was no chance of Sherriff's mistaking himself for Britain's answer to America's Tennessee Williams or Arthur Miller. His dramatic work was humble stuff, sometimes dull and often safe

The same criticisms have been made of Sherriff's work as a scriptwriter for the film industry. As his career took off after *Journey's End*, and as cinema took over from live theatre as the most popular form of entertainment, Sherriff was in demand. He began work on in Hollywood on a scripting of H.G. Wells's novel *The Invisible Man* (1933) but in 1936 turned down a contract from Universal Studios to write three screenplays at $25,000 each (an enormous sum in those days) in order that he could attend Oxford University as a mature student. He did however complete an adaptation of James Hilton's sentimental best-seller about an English public school-teacher, *Goodbye Mr Chips* (1939) whose life of service is seen as something to admire. Sherriff was nominated for an Oscar for his screenplay. The recurring sense of R.C. Sherriff as a patriotic writer is apparent, too, in *That Hamilton Woman* (1941), a propaganda film about an eighteenth century British hero Admiral Lord Horatio Nelson, whose patriotic speeches in the film – attributed some said to Winston Churchill rather than Sherriff – struck a chord with the cinema-going public in the Second World War. It helped that Nelson was played by Laurence Olivier, the original Captain Stanhope in 1928, now a big box-office star with his wife, Vivien Leigh, who also appeared in the film.

One obvious theme which these films share is what it means to be British – personally but also in terms of values and places. It is quite a narrow vision based, as we have seen in *Journey's End*, in part on ideas about fair play, doing one's duty, not making a fuss. It is one which also crops up in *Mrs Miniver* (1942) another Hollywood-produced film to which Sherriff contributed. This is about a British family in war-time who, as in *Journey's End*, are represented by the middle-classes inhabiting a cosy rural world of vicarage tea-parties and baking. During the course of the film, Ms Miniver, the heroine does her 'bit' by capturing a German airman. In the film's finale in a bombed church the vicar encourages his congregation to fight for victory against the Nazis after which they sing 'Onward Christian Soldiers' and the camera shifts to a shot of RAF bombers. The film won the Oscar for Best Picture despite seeming clichéd and sentimental. One film critic found it:

> Full of ghastly caricatures meant to represent the workers of Britain while at the other end of the social scale the Minivers themselves are portrayed as the backbone of the country – the comfortable, easy-going middle-class ... A few years ago you may remember how this class saved Britain from disaster by putting [Samuel] Baldwin into

power and applauding Munich . . . While Mrs Miniver and
her ilk drifted uselessly around village flower shows . . . nine
out of ten men in Jarrow were out of work . . . and now we
are asked to applaud this useless baggage . . . to represent a
nation at war.

Sunday Pictorial, 1 May 1942

This review is harsh but is worth quoting because parts of it
are very similar to negative criticisms made of *Journey's End*
by writers like Sean O'Casey (see p.83). These were that
Sherriff has a narrow, sentimental, social vision; is superficial;
is only interested in the stiff-upper lipped officer class; that he
can only see working-class characters like Mason, the cook in
Journey's End, in one-dimensional stereotypes (if he thinks
about them at all); that the basis of Britain's strength is the
country's public schools like Eton and Harrow. Of course, in
Mrs Miniver, this version of war-time Britain was what many
people felt was needed – a portrayal of how the country was
pulling together – and the film's writers were seen to have
reached new heights of patriotism. This idea was cemented a
decade later in Sherriff's scripting of another war film, *The
Dam Busters* (1955), the most-popular film in Britain in 1955,
which re-creates the real-life story of Operation Chastise when
in 1943 the RAF attacked German dams with the newly-
invented 'bouncing-bomb'. Yet these attacks on an outlook
that came to be seen as nationalistic, simplistic and old-
fashioned gradually began to be levelled at Sherriff's other
works too, rapidly displacing them as pieces worthy of
admiration, and causing people to see them as shallow and
unsophisticated pieces of writing. For the succeeding generation
of critics and theatre practitioners in the 1950s and 1960s like
Joan Littlewood, whose Theatre Workshop created a more
obviously angry play *Oh! What a Lovely War* in 1963,
Sherriff's work – even *Journey's End* – seemed very safe and
unadventurous in its attitudes

As literary lives go, few can have got off to such a good start
as Sherriff's, especially in the 1930s and 1940s. In old age he

continued to write plays including *The Long Sunset* (1955) about the last days of the Roman occupation of Britain, and *A Shred of Evidence* (1960), a thriller which took up another of his favourite themes: how a man behaves when facing disaster. Yet, by the end of the 1950s, Sherriff's career as a popular playwright and published author seems to have fizzled out. It may be that the books did not sell or he got discouraged or was simply ready to retire. His attempt to counterbalance this by writing novels did not seem to have come to much and few people these days have heard of the novels *King John's Treasure* (1954), *The Wells of St Mary's* (1962) or *The Seige of Swayne Castle* (1973). So gradually Sherriff retired from public view, perhaps having found something better to do (he was a keen archaeologist). People gradually forgot about this once-famous writer who went on living in Surrey until he died on 13 November 1975 aged 79.

Things to do

After reading this brief account of Sherriff's life and works, are there aspects you feel are relevant to your understanding of *Journey's End?* Or would you argue that none of this really matters to how the play should be interpreted?

James Whale (original director)

When he agreed to direct *Journey's End* in 1928, it was partly James Whale's vision of the play and its realization on stage which led to its success. Whale wanted the play to stand up to the scrutiny of veterans who knew the experience of war and would see the play as a medium to convey that truth to others. Born in Dudley, in 1889, he, like Sherriff, had served in the army during the war. Holding the rank of Second Lieutenant in the Worcester Infantry, Whale had also fought on the Western Front but had been captured and held as prisoner of war for almost a year and a half. In 1928 Whale was working as an actor and set designer but he was not an experienced director and was not first choice. However, Matthew Norgate of the Incorporated Stage Society thought Whale would be able to appreciate one of the play's central themes which was, as Norgate saw it, 'the disintegration of good and honourable men exposed over time to the most hopeless and brutal of circumstances' (quoted in James Curtis, *James Whale*, 53).

Whale was also responsible for the set design. He tried to capture a sense of claustrophobia felt by the men living underground – the earth propped up above their heads but likely to fall down at any minute. Whale wanted the dugout to convey not only a sense of protection but of imprisonment. The heavy timbers on the ceiling gave an impression of a heavy weight bearing down on the space. R.C. Sherriff praised Whale's design: 'There may have never been a dugout like this one, but any man who had lived in the trenches would say, "This is it: this is what it was like"' (quoted in *Curtis*, 54). Sherriff's point was that the set was clearly not real, or even accurate, but contained enough features that men who had served would recognize. This included trying to re-create the sound of war in ways which seem very basic now but seem to have been effective at the time: canes hit together created the sound of a machine gun; firecrackers were detonated in a large iron tank which then echoed round the theatre giving an impression of bombing. Whale wanted the audience to flinch every time they heard a shell explode outside the dugout, the shock interrupting the joking, the eating and the small routines that keep the soldiers stable. A big drum hanging from a beam was sounded to make the noise of distant gunfire.

In addition, Whale was responsible for casting. He did not want 'star' actors because he felt that they would overshadow the character they were playing. We might think of what happens when we see famous Hollywood actors in films. Often we admire their acting but we are still conscious that they – Tom Cruise or Meryl Streep – are playing a role. Their own personality and skill comes through. In contrast, if we do not know the actor we are often more likely to focus on the character in the film – or play. With *Journey's End*, Whale wanted the audience to see soldiers in a dug out – not famous actors pretending to be soldiers. In the first production, Laurence Olivier, later to become acknowledged as the twentieth century's greatest actor, was cast as Stanhope. Aged twenty-one, Olivier was the right age and was good-looking, able to convey Stanhope's charisma. He was also of course, too young to have fought in the war himself and did not understand some of the action or dialogue. According to one story he complained of *Journey's End*: 'There's nothing but meals in it.' Whale apparently replied: 'That's about all there was to think about in Flanders in the war' (quoted in *Curtis*, 55). Olivier did not continue with the play when it opened for its commercial run in 1929, opting instead to take the glamorous title role in an adaptation of the famous adventure novel about the French Foreign Legion, *Beau Geste*. An unknown actor, Colin Clive, replaced him and achieved an enormous success in the role.

The success of *Journey's End* in London in 1929 led to Whale's being invited to Hollywood to direct the film version for Universal Studios. These studios were also making a film of *All Quiet on the Western Front*. Afterwards Whale settled in Hollywood achieving renown as the director of horror films including *Frankenstein* (1931) and *The Bride of Frankenstein* (1935) as well as twenty-two others including *Show Boat* (1936) and *The Man in the Iron Mask* (1939). As his directorial career petered out in the 1940s, Whale became increasingly frustrated. He committed suicide in 1957. Whale's final days are evoked in the film *Gods and Monsters* (1995) which features Ian Mckellen as Whale.

Things to do

James Whale's films often feature an interest in characters who are imprisoned (figuratively and/or literally), e.g. the monster in *Frankenstein*. How are these interests apparent in *Journey's End*?

CHAPTER THREE

Writing About the Play

Although the exact questions asked in examinations will vary each year, overall they will always be asking you to demonstrate your possession of certain key skills and knowledge about the text you have studied. For example, you will always need to be able to show that you can:

> evaluate texts, providing informed personal response to what is read;

> analyse the techniques used by a writer to achieve specific purposes and effects;

> relate texts to their social, historical, cultural and literary contexts;

> compare and contrast texts (with reference to their contexts, themes, development of characterization, styles and literary qualities);

> write effectively about the texts, maintaining an appropriate discursive and literary style;

> use relevant quotation, detailed textual references and illustrative examples in writing to explore points of view.[1]

---

[1] Source: UK Government English literature GCSE subject content and assessment objectives (2015).

There are different ways of doing all these. Some of them, such as developing a personal response, are things that you need to develop over a period of time and as you revisit the literary texts you are studying. Try and take every opportunity to discuss the texts. Studying literature should involve exchanging ideas with other people; this will help you decide what *you* think about a particular play, novel or poem.

This section aims to give you some suggestions about how to become more effective at writing about *Journey's End* when faced with a written assignment such as an essay.

Preparation

Ensure that you know what the question asks. It is a good idea to choose a question that interests you as this will help motivate your work.

Resources

Your main resource will be the play text itself. It is *essential* that you re-read it, making note of any passages, conversations and ideas which are particularly relevant to your topic.

Constructing an argument

It is easy to take essay writing for granted rather than think about what kind of skills it demands, or what the finished article itself should ideally look like. Your written answer is at heart an *argument*. Unfortunately, answers often consist of a collection of interesting but only loosely related points which do not work side-by-side to form a coherent whole. They often take the form of 'shopping lists' of individual points, lacking the structure of an overarching *thesis* (argument).

It is this thesis which is essential. To write a good answer you need to have a clear sense from the beginning of what it is you are trying to achieve over the course of the pages of your essay. You should be able to summarize, in a sentence or two, what the point of your essay is: what argument it is setting out to demonstrate.

Try to achieve balance. You are not writing a political tract and you should try acknowledging alternative viewpoints. Aim for an informed review: summarize as fairly as possible the rival positions on the topic of your essay, give the pros and cons associated with each, examine the evidence of the text(s) and then try to arrive at what you think is the most satisfactory conclusions.

Pitching the level of your writing can be difficult. It is often useful to write as if your intended audience is an intelligent student who has no specialized knowledge of your topic. Do not assume that this audience knows all of the relevant material already, but equally, do not be patronising. Nor do you need to re-tell the story of the play; this just wastes time.

Personal opinion. Do not be afraid of giving your opinion. This is what you should be doing but you need to back it up with some evidence. Try and avoid saying 'I think'. This can sound weak. If you are offering strong textual evidence you do not need to say this. Simply by offering the evidence you have shown what you think.

Textual evidence

You will need to refer to or quote from the text in order to provide evidence for the claim you are making. Be careful how you do this. One of the mistakes students make is to plonk a quote into the middle of a sentence without saying *who* is speaking and in *what* context. They think that the reader can work it out. This is not helpful. You need to make it easy for your reader to follow your argument at all times. One good way to do this is to introduce your quotes. This is an example:

When the Colonel says goodbye to Raleigh just before the raid he tells him to 'just go in like blazes. Grab hold of the

first Boche you see and bundle him across here. One'll do,
but bring more if you see any handy.'

In an examination in which you do not have access to the text,
you may find it easier to locate a quotation within a particular
moment of the play as is done here, rather than specifying the
exact scene it comes from.

Next, you need to make sure the quotation makes the point
you want it to, by making this clear to the reader. This means
providing an explanation of what the quotation reveals. For
example, you might say something like, 'In this exchange, the
Colonel shows his unwillingness to admit the real dangers of
the raid' or 'Here the Colonel can be seen trying to bolster
Raleigh's confidence, knowing this is his first experience of
fighting'. Whilst you should always explain the value of your
quotation in this way, you do not need to explain in detail your
thinking behind your choice. Students sometimes write things
like, 'I have chosen this quotation to show that the Colonel is
out of touch'. However this is very longwinded and looks
clumsy; you need to try and write succinctly. If the quote is a
powerful one, there should be no need to explain the workings
of your brain.

One of the things you will have to do in an examination
is to quote from the text from memory. However, the
examination is not only a test of what you know but rather of
how competently you can use your knowledge to answer
particular questions. You do not need to learn long chunks of
dialogue. It is better – and easier – to have some short quotes
that you can apply to more than one situation or sum up a
particular character. For example, you could learn a section
of the speech in which Stanhope describes No Man's Land as
'just an enormous plain, all churned up like a sea that's got
muddier and muddier till it's so still that it can't move' (45) to
illustrate (1) how Sherriff has characters describe for the
audience what the view is like from the trenches; (2) to indicate
Stanhope's state of mind; or (3) to suggest how the soldiers
are trapped.

Things to do

Choose and learn some quotations that illustrate:

- Each of the themes discussed in the **Themes** section of this Guide.

- A key trait of each of the play's characters.

- Key moments of tension or disagreement between the characters.

Analysing the playwright's technique

Examination criteria require you to analyse techniques used by a writer to achieve specific purposes and effects. In other words, you need to look at *what* they are communicating to an audience and *how* they are doing that. For example, at the end of Act One, the audience sees the depth of friendship between Stanhope and Osborne when the latter tucks Stanhope into bed. The audience have already seen Osborne defending Stanhope to Hardy at the beginning of the act but here his protective feelings are acted out as he '*firmly takes Stanhope by the arm and draws him over the bed . . . takes the blanket and pulls it over him*' (34). In the same section of the play the audience sees first-hand the extent of Stanhope's drinking. The audience has been told about it previously in the expository conversations. Now it is shown in full as stage directions show Stanhope pouring himself three drinks in a very short space of time, ending with him getting drunk. By now, the extent of Stanhope's addiction has been revealed to everyone with the exception of Raleigh.

Writing about character

You may be asked to consider how a character is presented within one scene of the play, or to consider a character's journey across the course of the whole play. Does a character change or remain the same?

There are several things to remember when writing about characters in plays. These are the main ones:

- Characters are not real people. They are constructs built by the author. The audience only knows what it sees and hears on stage.

- In a play text a character is *delivered* to an audience through stage directions and dialogue (see the section on 'Characters' in this guide). Dialogue is used to convey information about characters: what they say about themselves and what they think about things, but also what others say about them. *How* characters speak is another way of discovering something about them. Characters from a similar social, regional or class group often share a similar way of speaking. In Britain, the way in which characters educated at a boarding school in southern England speak and intermingle will be different from the ways of those of a group of Scottish fishermen. When writing about plays, this use of a collective form of speech is termed a *sociolect*.

- You should also think about the *function* of each character in the plot. Every character is there for a reason. For example, one reason why Sherriff introduces Raleigh into the play is to increase the pressure on Stanhope. It turns out that Raleigh knows a lot about Stanhope, including his relationship with his sister, and as a result has some power over him, even if he does not use it in the way Stanhope fears. One of his functions is to give insight into Stanhope's previous existence. 'I remember once at school he caught some chaps in a study with a bottle of whisky. Lord! the roof nearly blew off. He gave them a dozen each with a cricket stump' (19). We see how far Stanhope has fallen – he is now the one drinking – but Raleigh's comments also reveal (unintentionally) Stanhope's capacity for brutality. He is an unbending, unyielding figure who expects others to behave as he does.

- Raleigh's arrival in the dugout also invites a contrast between his wide-eyed, innocent attitude to the situation in which he finds himself and that of Stanhope. In Sherriff's plan for this play, Raleigh is a *foil* to Stanhope – they are two characters who invite comparison from the audience. Raleigh is also a foil to Osborne. There is another foil in the play in the person of Lieutenant Hibbert. As the play unfolds the audience sees how serving in the trenches has pushed Hibbert towards a nervous breakdown. He freely admits this and tries to avoid going into battle. As Stanhope admits his own fragile mental state and his own fears, our knowledge of Hibbert serves as a point of comparison and a means of understanding Stanhope's tremendous will power. It is worth pointing out that having characters as foils to one another is a reminder that what we are watching is not real life. In our everyday lives we do not have foils. So a foil is part of the artificially created world of the play and is there for the benefit of the audience.

Things to do

Pick a three-page extract from the play and list the different ways in which the characters are *delivered* to the audience. You could begin with Act One, from Raleigh's entrance beginning '*Mason leaves the dugout*' and ending with '*Osborne rouses himself and speaks briskly*' (16, 19).

Analysing the text

Often it can be tempting to try to answer the question simply by throwing in lots of facts about the play and what happens in it. This only doing half the job.

You need to remember that you can describe what happens on stage and what characters do and say but you need to analyse the significance of it all. So, you can say that Stanhope drinks a lot but this observation only really counts for much if you use it as a jumping off point for some wider analysis. This means you suggesting what your observation might mean or signify within the context of the play. For example, you might argue that Stanhope's drinking is a way of communicating the emotional strain he is under. However, it may be that there are several things you could say. For example, you might argue that the emphasis on Stanhope's drinking at the end of Act One is also an effective way to communicate his immaturity, particularly when viewed alongside Osborne's contrasting behaviour.

Things to do

Take the following descriptive statements and use them as a basis for further analysis:

1 In the opening of Act One, Hardy explains the rules of earwig racing to Osborne.

2 At the end of Act Three, Scene Two, Stanhope is outraged when Raleigh sits on Osborne's bed after his return from the raid.

3 When an injured Raleigh is brought down to the dugout, Stanhope wets his handkerchief and bathes Raleigh's face.

Connecting text to context

No literary text is written in isolation, they are all products of a particular culture and a particular historical moment. Some of the contexts for *Journey's End* were discussed earlier in this guide (see p. 16). In order to appreciate *Journey's End* fully you need to be conscious of these, not least its position as one of a number of texts which tried to re-present the experience of the First World War in the 1920s. You also need to understand something of the experience of soldiers in the First World War itself. However, you should be careful not to become too focused on these details at the expense of your engagement with the play itself. Sherriff said that he drew on personal experience in his writing of *Journey's End* but he was also writing a play, a piece of creative writing. So in writing about the play you can suggest certain personal and cultural influences that may have impacted on Sherriff, but you should put the play first. What you do not need to do is spend time discussing Sherriff's life in a long separate paragraph. Only introduce details about it if it seems relevant to the issue you are discussing at the time. Thus the play's use of military slang does presumably have its origins in Sherriff's war service but you do not need to go into lots of detail about this. Ultimately you are trying to demonstrate how context is integrally linked to the play, so it should be blended into the paragraph in which you are making this point.

Things to do

Imagine you are reading Act Three, Scene Two for the first time, having no knowledge about the play, who wrote it or when. Which sections of the scene would you have trouble understanding or have difficulty appreciating without additional knowledge? Is there any contextual information which would improve your understanding of the scene?

Five tips

1   Keep the style relatively formal. You are not writing an article in a popular newspaper. In general, slang expressions and clichés are not appropriate (e.g. 'the censorship of Raleigh's letter becomes a *hot potato*'). In everyday speech we tend to use a great number of contractions such 'I'll', 'won't', 'hadn't', 'she'd' and so forth. When you are writing an essay, you are using a more formal version of English so avoid contractions

2   Work on your errors. Everybody makes mistakes. The trick in writing is to try and avoid repeating them.

3   Conventionally, when we write about a text we do so in the present tense: 'In *Journey's End*, Sherriff *explores* the impact of warfare on a group of soldiers' and 'Raleigh *receives* a hostile welcome from Stanhope'. The crucial thing, however, is that you avoid mixing tenses unnecessarily. So avoid saying 'Raleigh *went* on a raid and Colonel *says* goodbye to him'.

4   Introductions. Always plan a clear, well-written introduction, which does not simply parrot or reiterate what the question states. It should also detail the broad sweep of your essay.

5   Conclusions. Time-permitting you should attempt to write a decent-sized conclusion. Do not, however, simply repeat what you have already said. Imagine you are a judge summing up a case. You need to offer an informed verdict in response to the set question.

Final thoughts

By the end of your course you should know *Journey's End* very well. Your knowledge about the play, and how it is structured and written, should enable you to discuss it with confidence. As a critic your opinions are as valuable as anybody else's.

Journey's End is a work which operates on different levels and provokes strong opinions. There is no right and wrong interpretation of it as long as you can provide evidence to back up your own reading of it.

A final piece of advice would be to take any opportunity to watch the play being performed – either live on stage or via filmed recordings. This way you will get some sense of what R.C. Sherriff envisaged and get a sense, too, of how each production will try to stress different aspects of the play.

BIBLIOGRAPHY

Archer, William. *Masks or Faces? A Study in the Psychology of Acting* (London: Longmans, 1888).

Bracco, Rosa Maria. *Merchants of Hope: British Middlebrow Writers and the First World War* (Oxford: Berg, 1993).

Brittain, Vera. 'War Service in Perspective', in G.A. Panichas (ed.), *Promise of Greatness: The War of 1914–1918* (London: Cassell, 1968), pp. 363–76.

Clark, Alan. *The Donkeys* (London: Hutchinson, 1961).

Curtis, James. *James Whale. A New World of Gods and Monsters* (Minnesota: University of Minneapolis, 2003).

Fone, Byrne. *A Road to Stonewall: Male Homosexuality and Homophobia in English and American Literature 1750–1969* (New York: Twayne, 1995).

Forster, E.M. *Aspects of the Novel* (1927) (Penguin, 2000).

Gatiss, Mark. *James Whale: A Biography* (New York: Cassell, 1995).

Gregory, Adrian. *Silence of Memory: Armistice Day 1919–1946* (Providence: Berg, 1994).

Grein, J.T. *The New World of the Theatre 1923–1924* (London: Martin Hopkinson & Co, 1924).

Howard, Michael. *The First World War. A Very Short Introduction* (Oxford: Oxford University Press, 2007).

Hynes, Samuel. *A War Imagined: The First World War and English Culture* (London: Pimlico, 1992).

Kosok, Heinz. *The Theatre of War: The First World War in British and Irish Drama* (Basingstoke: Palgrave Macmillan, 2007).

Napper, Laurence. 'That Filth from which the glamour is not even departed: Adapting *Journey's End*', in *Modern British Drama on Screen*, ed. R. Barton Palmer (Cambridge: Cambridge University Press, 2013), pp. 12–30.

Onions, John. *English Fiction and Drama of the Great War, 1918–39* (Basingstoke: Macmillan, 1990).

Page, Norman. *Speech in the English Novel* (London: Macmillan, 1988).

Parfitt, George. *Fiction of the First World War* (London: Faber, 1988).

Priestly, J.B. *Margin Released* (London: Methuen, 1962).

Roper, Michael. 'Between manliness and masculinity: the "war generation" and the psychology of fear in Britain, 1914–1970', *Journal of British Studies*, 44:2 (2005), pp. 343–63.

Sheffield, Gary. *Forgotten Victory: The First World War: Myths and Realities* (London: Headline, 2002).

Shepherd, Simon, and Mick Wallis. *Studying Plays* (London: Bloomsbury, 2010).

Sherriff, R.C. *Journey's End* (1929) (Penguin Modern Classics, 2000).

—— *No Leading Lady. An Autobiography* (London: Gollancz, 1968).

Smith, Angela. *The Second Battlefield. Women, Modernism and the First World War* (Manchester: Manchester University Press, 2000).

Soames, Mary (ed.). *Speaking for Themselves: The Personal Letters of Winston and Clementine Churchill* (London: Black Swan, 1999).

Taylor, Martin. *Lads: Love Poetry of the Trenches* (1989).

Trout, Steven. 'Glamorous Melancholy: R.C. Sherriff's *Journeys End*', *War, Literature and the Arts*. 5:2 (1993), pp. 1–19.

Winter, Jay, and Antoine Prost, *The Great War in History: Debates and Controversies, 1914 to the Present* (Cambridge: Cambridge University Press, 2005).

Woolf, Virginia. *The Letters of Virginia Woolf, 1912–1922*. Ed Nigel Nicolson (London: Hogarth Press, 1986).

INDEX